Girl, L

Self-Love Secrets for Teen Girls

Gain Self-Confidence, Release Fear of Judgment, & Stop Caring What Others Think

Brenda Emerson

© **Copyright 2024 by Brenda Emerson -**

All rights reserved.

Disclaimer Notice:

Please note the information contained within this document is for educational and entertainment purposes only. All effort has been executed to present accurate, up to date, and reliable, complete information. No warranties of any kind are declared or implied. Readers acknowledge that the author is not engaging in the rendering of legal, financial, medical or professional advice. The content within this book has been derived from various sources. Please consult a licensed professional before attempting any techniques outlined in this book. By reading this document, the reader agrees that under no circumstances is the author responsible for any losses, direct or indirect, which are incurred as a result of the use of information contained within this document, including, but not limited to, — errors, omissions, or inaccuracies.

Table of Contents

Looking to make meaningful friendships? As a bonus, I've included a mini-guide that shares 7 simple tips to help teen girls find their tribe!

<u>Click here to download your free guide</u>, or scan the QR code.

Introduction: Why Self-Love Matters

Navigating your way through high school hallways buzzing with gossip and scrolling through social media feeds showcasing seemingly perfect lives can feel overwhelming, right? You're constantly bombarded with unwritten rules about fitting in, along with pressure to rack up likes and approval. It's like you're climbing a mountain where the peaks are perfect beauty, outstanding success, and ultimate popularity —it's exhausting. Every day seems to bring new challenges and fresh doubts about whether you're good enough.

But here's the good news amidst all the chaos: self-love can be your secret weapon. And no, it's not just some passing trend—it's your power move against a culture that often tries to chip away at your self-esteem. Self-love is about recognizing that your true value isn't measured by likes or external approval. It comes from your own acts of kindness, your resilience in the face of challenges, and your unwavering belief in your worth. Remember, you're more than enough, just as you are.

Picture this: Emily, a freshman with eager eyes, nervously walks through the school gates on her first day. The air is buzzing with excitement as she sees her classmates chatting effortlessly, as if they've done it a million times before. Their laughter fills the halls, creating a cheerful melody. But as Emily tries to find her place among them, doubts start to creep in. She wants to belong, to feel accepted, but she's not sure how. Every day, she carefully chooses what to share online, hoping it will make her seem cool and likable. Despite her efforts, she can't shake the feeling that she's not good enough, that she'll never truly fit in.

Emily's story is relatable to many teenagers struggling with self-worth and confidence. Studies show that this is a widespread issue, especially among girls. Shocking statistics from the Dove Self-Esteem Project reveal that 7 out of 10 girls feel inadequate, believing they fall short in different areas of their lives. Social media makes this feeling worse by bombarding them with perfect images and stories. These platforms create an unrealistic standard that leaves many feeling unworthy and unsure of themselves. It's like being lost in a world where everyone seems perfect, and it's hard to find where you fit in.

What if I revealed to you that confidence, resilience, and inner peace are all right there within you, waiting to be unlocked? Self-love isn't just some passing trend or a snappy slogan—it's a game-changer, a total game-changer! Renowned psychologist Dr. Kristin Neff puts it perfectly: self-compassion means treating yourself with the same kindness you'd show a dear friend in need. It's about embracing your flaws, celebrating your uniqueness, and realizing that your worth doesn't hinge on anyone else's opinion. Self-love isn't a luxury—it's a must-have for your personal growth and well-being, urging you to dive into a journey of self-discovery and empowerment like no other!

Take a moment to envision a delicate flower unfolding its petals in the sunlight. Like this bloom's intricate needs, our inner selves require nourishment, care, and nurturing to thrive. Just as a flower depends on soil, water, and sunlight, our spirits crave love, acceptance, and kindness to grow. When we cultivate self-love within ourselves, we not only improve our own well-being but also radiate positivity and authenticity to those around us. It's like a ripple effect, where our inner confidence spreads outward, inspiring others on their own paths of self-discovery and empowerment. By nurturing our self-love, we become guiding lights, illuminating the way for others to find their own inner strength and fulfillment.

Let's dive into the research highlighting the incredible significance of self-love—it's not just some fleeting idea that feels nice, but an absolutely crucial element for our mental well-being and toughness. Studies conducted by the American Psychological Association reveal some seriously eye-opening insights. Brace yourself for this: folks who actively practice self-love and self-compassion?

They're rocking notably lower levels of anxiety, depression, and stress. Yeah, you heard that right! It's like having a superpower shield against life's toughest moments. By building this nurturing and supportive relationship with ourselves, we're basically constructing an impenetrable fortress of inner strength. Picture it: a fortress where we can weather any storm and embrace every joy that comes our way with arms wide open. This isn't just about a temporary mood lift—it's about laying down a rock-solid foundation of self-worth and self-acceptance that anchors us through the crazy rollercoaster ride of life.

So, why is self-love so incredibly crucial for teenage girls? Well, let's break it down. We live in a world where girls are bombarded non-stop with messages telling them they're not good enough. It's like a constant storm of negativity raining down on them every day. But in the midst of all that chaos, self-love becomes their saving grace—a guiding light that helps them navigate through the tough times of being a teenager. It's like a rebellion against all those impossible standards society tries to force on them. Self-love shouts out loud that their worth isn't defined by how many likes they get on social media or how trendy they are. It's about taking back control of their own stories, standing tall in their own skin, and saying, "Hey, I'm enough just as I am." Choosing self-love is like standing up against a tidal wave of pressure to fit in, showing the world your strength and resilience in the face of it all.

As we eagerly flip through the pages ahead, get ready to dive headfirst into an exhilarating journey of self-discovery and empowerment! It's like embarking on a thrilling quest, powered by the unstoppable forces of compassion, authenticity, and fierce self-love. Side by side, we'll navigate through the intricate layers of our inner worlds, peeling them back to uncover the brilliant essence that lies within. Along this epic adventure, we'll shatter the illusions and misconceptions that cloud our sense of self-worth, revealing the raw, unfiltered truth waiting to be embraced. Equipped with a toolbox bursting with practical tips and strategies, we'll arm ourselves to bravely confront the challenges life throws our way. And let's not forget to revel in the sheer magnificence of embracing ourselves fully, quirks and all, recognizing that **our uniqueness is our superpower**! So, let's charge forward with hearts wide open and unyielding determination, fueled by the limitless potential that resides within each and every one of us!

Audre Lorde, a well-known writer and activist, once said, "Taking care of myself is not self-indulgence, it is self-preservation, and that is an act of political warfare." By practicing self-love and self-care, we stand up against the things that try to break us down and make us feel less important. Let's move forward together, strengthened by our compassion, empowered by our inner bravery, and confident in our own value. Together, we can light the way to self-love, leaving our doubts and fears behind, and embracing the amazing potential within each of us.

Chapter 1: Understanding Yourself

The Teenage Metamorphosis: Understanding the Transition from Childhood to Adolescence

As you step from childhood into your teen years, you enter a really important and sometimes confusing phase. This is when you start to see lots of changes—not just in your body but in your mind and emotions too. It's a time when you really start to figure out who you are.

During these years, your body changes faster than it ever has before. Thanks to a rush of hormones, you might feel like you're on a rollercoaster. Dr. Sarah Jane, a well-known pediatrician, points out how big this period of growth is. This can feel pretty overwhelming at times, but it's also a chance to really get to know yourself and embrace all these new parts of who you're becoming.

Going through puberty can feel like you're on a non-stop emotional rollercoaster. Just ask Frankie, who was only 13 when she started noticing big changes. One day, she looked in the mirror and barely recognized herself. "Suddenly, I didn't recognize myself anymore," she says about seeing her new curves, dealing with acne, shooting up in height, and her weight changing unexpectedly. It's pretty common to feel shaken up as your body changes. These changes aren't just about how you look; they make you rethink how you feel about yourself, which can really shake your confidence.

As you go through these changes, remember, your brain is changing right alongside your body. Dr. Lisa Miller, a psychologist who works with teens, explains that it's not just your emotions that are all over the place. Your brain is also developing fast, especially in the areas that help you make decisions, control impulses, and handle your feelings. As you figure out who you are and how to deal with people, you might feel super happy one moment and totally down the next. Feeling this way is completely normal and part of growing up. It helps shape how you see yourself and others, and it sets the stage for all your future relationships and personal growth.

Sarah, now in her high school sophomore year, reflects on the emotional rollercoaster ride that characterizes the teenage years. "One moment," she recounts, "I'd be laughing with my friends, and the next, I'd feel overwhelmed by sadness or anxiety." These abrupt shifts in mood are a frequent occurrence as girls navigate the challenges of peer pressure, academic stress, and the quest for self-identity.

During these changes, the craving for independence becomes more apparent. Dr. Elizabeth Smith, an expert in adolescent psychiatry, explains, "Teenage girls often want to be independent to show their uniqueness and find their place in the world." This desire for freedom can lead to rebelling against parents, trying out new identities, and seeking out new experiences.

For parents, witnessing their daughters undergo these changes can be a whirlwind of emotions. Laura, a mother of two teenage girls, reflects, "It's like witnessing a metamorphosis right in front of my eyes—from carefree children to independent young women." Indeed, parenting during adolescence demands a delicate dance of support, guidance, and understanding as girls navigate this transformative period.

The Power of Your Thoughts: Understanding Self-Talk.

Think of yourself walking through a hallway in your mind. It's kind of dark and mysterious, with shadows all around whispering stuff like "you can't do this" or "you're not good enough." These whispers? They're actually your own voice talking back to you, saying things that aren't really true but feel super real. But guess what? You're not walking through this spooky mental hallway alone. I'm right here with you, ready to help you figure this whole thing out and show those negative whispers who's boss. This part of the book? It's made just for you, a teenage girl who's way tougher and more awesome than she might think.

Imagine this hallway is like the hallways at school, but instead of locker noise, there are those whispering shadows. They seem to follow you around, echoing your deepest doubts. It's as if your own thoughts have turned into these little ghosts that haunt you, telling you all the reasons why you can't achieve your dreams or be who you want to be.

But here's the cool part: just like in those adventure movies where the hero learns how to overcome their fears, you're about to learn how to do the same with these whispering doubts. This chapter is like your guidebook or your map to beating those negative voices. It's here to show you that, yes, those whispers can be pretty convincing, but they don't get to decide what you're capable of. You do.

We're going to take this journey step by step, together. I'll show you how to spot those whispers, understand why they're there, and then, most importantly, how to quiet them down so you can hear your own true voice— the one that knows how strong and capable you really are. Think of each tip and strategy as a tool, kind of like a flashlight or a key, something that can help you clear the shadows and light up that hallway, making it a place where you're in control.

And hey, as we walk through this together, remember that feeling a bit scared or unsure is totally normal. What matters is that you're brave enough to start this journey, to learn more about yourself and how to turn those "I can't" whispers into "I definitely can." This chapter is all about finding that inner strength and confidence that's been there all along, just waiting for you to tap into it.

Understanding the Voices Inside Us

Let's talk about Sandra for a moment. Picture her as someone who's really smart and full of big dreams, kinda like you. When it's her turn to speak up in class, though, there's this little voice inside her head that starts saying she's going to mess it all up. It turns out, according to Dr. Lisa Damour, who's pretty much an expert on what teens go through, this happens to a lot of us. In fact, 9 out of 10 girls hear this kind of voice, which can make us see ourselves in a pretty harsh light.

Originally, this inner voice was supposed to be helpful, kind of like a built-in warning system to keep us from making mistakes. But when you're a teenager, trying to figure out who you are while dealing with all kinds of pressure (yep, including the crazy world of social media), this voice can start sounding more like an enemy than a friend.

Back in the day, this voice helped our ancestors stay out of trouble by making them think twice before doing something risky. Nowadays, though, the challenges you face are a lot different, especially with the added pressure from social media, where it feels like everyone's watching and judging your every move. This can make that voice in your head get pretty loud and negative, focusing more on what you think you can't do instead of all the amazing things you can do.

For someone like Sandra, or maybe even for you, this isn't just something that stays inside your head. It can stop you from raising your hand in class even when you know the answer, keep you from trying out for a team or club, or make you hold back your great ideas when you're working with friends. This voice, which is supposed to help, ends up holding you back instead.

But here's the deal: realizing that almost everyone has this voice can actually make you feel a bit better about it. It's not just you— it's a common thing, and it doesn't mean there's something wrong with you. It's like turning on the light in a dark room and seeing that what you thought was something scary is actually just a chair. Once you know it's there and understand what it's all about, you can start learning how to deal with it better.

Getting a handle on this voice isn't about shutting it up completely. It's about learning to listen to it in a way that helps instead of hurts. It means noticing when it's being too harsh and finding ways to talk back to it with some kindness and truth about yourself. The journey from letting this voice control you to you being in control of it can be tough but also pretty rewarding. It's about turning that voice from a critic that drags you down into one that's more like a coach, cheering you on.

Tackling the Inner Critic: Emily's Space Dream

Jasmine, who dreams of floating among the stars as an astronaut. But every time she thinks about it, a voice in her head says, "You're not smart enough for that." Sounds familiar, right? Sadly, this kind of self-doubt is something a lot of us deal with, especially girls. There's a ton of studies out there that show how common it is to struggle with feeling good about ourselves because we've got this constant negative chatter going on in our heads. Wanting to be liked and accepted is a big deal, and the fear of messing up or being rejected can feel really intense. That's when the inner critic starts to get really loud, picking on every little insecurity.

And then there's social media, which doesn't help. It's like a highlight reel where everyone only posts their best moments, making it seem like they're living perfect lives. Our inner critic takes one look at that and uses it as proof that we're not doing as great, which just isn't true.

But why do we give these negative thoughts so much power? Part of it is just habit. If you've always reacted to mistakes or criticism by being hard on yourself, it starts to feel normal. And then society has all these expectations about what girls should be like, which can make you doubt yourself even more.

Fighting back against the inner critic isn't easy, but it's totally possible. It starts with realizing that the critical voice in your head isn't the boss of you. You can learn to spot when it's being overly negative and challenge those thoughts. There are strategies, like what you might find in therapy, that teach you how to swap out those negative thoughts with ones that are more positive and true.

Being kind to yourself is a big part of beating the inner critic, too. Remember, everyone makes mistakes and has things they're not perfect at, and that's okay. It doesn't make you any less awesome.

And don't forget, having friends and people who support you can make a huge difference. They can help remind you of your strengths and cheer you on when your inner critic is trying to bring you down.

For Jasmine, and for anyone else with a big dream, getting past the inner critic is a big step toward making that dream a reality. It's about learning to see yourself in a better light, focusing on your strengths and the things you're passionate about, instead of getting stuck on what you're afraid of or what you think you can't do.

Beating the Negative Talk: How to Turn Down the Volume on Self-Doubt

Starting to beat the negative talk in your head begins with one important thing: being aware. It's all about noticing when those downer thoughts pop up and why. Take Anna's story, for example. She loves playing volleyball, but she noticed something tough – every time she made a mistake during a game, her mind would go off on her, making her feel really bad about herself, way beyond just the mistake she made. When she realized this was happening, it was a wake-up call for her to start fighting back against those negative thoughts.

Being super kind to yourself, kind of like how you would treat your best friend, is a huge deal here. Messed up? It's totally okay – everyone does. Going after perfection all the time is like trying to catch the wind with your hands – it's just not going to happen, and you'll just end up tired and frustrated.

There are so many ways to push back against the negative stuff we sometimes tell ourselves. One way is to challenge those downer thoughts head-on and replace them with positive ones. It's not about ignoring the bad stuff; it's about reminding yourself of the good stuff, too. Writing down how you're feeling, practicing being in the moment (mindfulness), and giving yourself props for the awesome things you do can all help build you up.

Journaling is kind of like having a conversation with yourself on paper. It lets you get all those thoughts out of your head and see them from a different angle. It can be a great way to deal with tough emotions and start to see things more clearly.

Mindfulness is another tool in your kit. It's about being fully present and not judging your thoughts too harshly. Through practices like meditation, you can learn to watch your thoughts come and go without getting too caught up in them. This gives you the space to choose kindness over criticism.

Affirmations are positive things you can say about yourself to boost your mood and confidence. Think of them like your personal cheerleading squad, reminding you of your strengths, what you've accomplished, and all the cool stuff that makes you, you.

Shining a Light Together

The stories we've been sharing - think of Sarah, Jasmine, and Anna - are a bit like looking into a mirror, aren't they? You might see bits of your own story reflected back at you. What's really cool, though, is that these stories aren't just about the tough times. They're brimming with hope. It's like they're telling us, "Hey, if they can make it through, so can we." And that's what we're here for, to walk through this together, learning how to treat ourselves with a bit more kindness and a lot more patience, and to gather up the courage to face those not-so-friendly shadows.

There's this powerful thing Maya Angelou once said, "You may not control all the events that happen to you, but you can decide not to be reduced by them." That's pretty huge, right? It's like she's nudging us to dig deep, find our strength, and strut out of those shadows with a newfound confidence.

And guess what? This is just the beginning. We're about to dive into a whole bunch of ways to pump up your confidence, make you even more resilient, and get you loving yourself so much that those doubting whispers don't stand a chance.

Visualize transforming that creepy, doubt-filled hallway in your mind into a bright path glowing with light, where every step you take makes you feel a bit more like the superhero you are.

Chapter 2: The Beauty of Imperfection

In today's world, where Instagram filters and Photoshop make everything look perfect, showing off our real selves, with all our so-called flaws, feels almost like breaking the rules. It's like everyone expects us to hide what makes us different, to only show the polished, picture-perfect versions of ourselves. But here's a secret: it's those exact differences, those imperfections, that make us truly beautiful. This chapter isn't just about being okay with not being perfect; it's about throwing a party for all the things that make us unique, turning what everyone else calls weaknesses into our coolest features.

We're diving deep into why our so-called flaws are actually something to cheer about. In a sea of copies, it's our unique traits that make us stand out. Those laugh lines from too many good times, scars from our adventures, or the way we snort when we laugh—these aren't mistakes. They're like little stories about who we are and what we've been through, stories that no one else can tell but us.

But this isn't just about learning to live with these parts of ourselves; it's about seeing them as badges of honor. It's about flipping the script and seeing our quirks not as things we have to deal with but as our superpowers. Imagine if we all started showing off what makes us different instead of hiding it. That would be the real game-changer.

In this chapter, we're not only going to talk about why we should stop sweating our imperfections but also how they can be our secret weapons. Every freckle, every unique laugh, and every odd habit is a piece of the puzzle that makes you, you. And trust me, the world is way more interesting with you being your genuine, imperfect self.

So, as we go through this together, think of this chapter as your guide to rocking your quirks with pride. We'll look at how seeing the beauty in our so-called flaws can actually make us feel more confident, how it can be a relief to stop chasing the impossible dream of being perfect, and how our differences can bring us closer to others.

Embracing our imperfections doesn't mean giving up on trying to be our best selves; it means redefining what "best" means. It means recognizing that being real, being authentically us, is way cooler than any filter or edit could ever make us. By the end of this, I hope you'll be ready to celebrate every part of yourself, knowing that it's your unique combination of traits that makes you awesome.

Let's Talk About Being Perfectly Imperfect

Have you ever felt like you're constantly trying to be perfect but it just doesn't exist? Well, you're not alone. The truth is, perfection is like a mirage. It's something that seems real from a distance but when you get up close, it's nowhere to be found. This whole idea of needing to be perfect all the time can really wear you down and steal the fun out of life.

Now, let me introduce you to something pretty awesome called *kintsugi*. It's this art form from Japan where people take broken pottery and fix it up with gold. Instead of hiding the cracks, they fill them in with gold and make them stand out. The end result? The pottery isn't just fixed; it's given a whole new kind of beauty, celebrating its history and its journey. Imagine if we started looking at ourselves and each other like that. Instead of hiding our so-called flaws, we could highlight them and see them as something that makes us uniquely beautiful.

Chasing after perfection is like running on a treadmill that never stops. It's tiring and, honestly, pretty impossible. It's like the world keeps telling you to jump higher, only to move the bar up just as you're about to reach it. That's no way to live. It's time to hop off that treadmill and really take in the view from where you already are.

Kintsugi isn't just about pottery; it's a whole way of seeing life. It shows us that the things about us that aren't "perfect" are what make us stand out. The quirky things you do that make you, you, or even the tough times you've been through that have taught you something important - they're all golden. They're what make your story yours.

Breaking free from the idea that we need to be perfect can totally change how you see yourself and the world. It's about ditching that voice in your head that tells you you're not good enough because you're not like someone else. It's about celebrating the real, the raw, and what makes you uniquely you. It's finding joy in the fact that no one else has the same mix of experiences, challenges, and quirks as you do. And that's pretty cool.

Embracing Our Flaws: Stories That Inspire

Everyone has something about them that's unique, but sometimes it can feel like these unique bits are more like flaws we need to hide. Yet, there are some pretty cool stories out there about people who've taken what they thought were flaws and turned them into their biggest strengths.

Let's talk about Jess, a 10th grader who really didn't like her freckles. She used to spend a lot of time trying to cover them up with makeup because she thought they made her look weird. But then, Jess, who loves to paint and draw, started seeing her freckles in a whole new light. To her, they began to look like natural spots of beauty that an artist might add to a painting to make it more interesting. So, she changed up how she did her makeup to show off her freckles instead of hiding them. This small change made a huge difference in how she saw herself and pretty soon, her freckles became her favorite feature.

Then there's Alex, who found reading out loud in class really tough because of her dyslexia. Words seemed to jump around on the page, making it hard for her to keep up. But, this struggle actually helped Alex discover she's amazing at thinking in pictures and solving problems in creative ways, skills that are super valuable and not everyone has. Alex started to see her dyslexia not as a problem, but as something that gave her a special edge.

Stories like Jess's and Alex's show us something important: what we might think of as our flaws can actually be what makes us stand out. Instead of seeing these unique parts of ourselves as something bad, we can learn to see them as our superpowers.

Their experiences teach us to look at ourselves differently, to appreciate the things that make us who we are, even if they're not what everyone expects. It's about understanding that the stuff that makes us different can also make us pretty amazing. Jess and Alex remind us to be proud of what makes us unique and to use it to our advantage. After all, it's our so-called flaws that can turn out to be our greatest strengths.

Understanding Self-Acceptance

Psychologists and experts have been digging into how accepting ourselves and not stressing over being perfect affects our lives. Dr. Kristin Neff, who knows a ton about being kind to ourselves, tells us that being okay with our imperfections can actually make our lives happier and way less stressful. She points out that trying to be perfect all the time can make us anxious, sad, and scared of messing up. On the flip side, treating ourselves with kindness can help us feel stronger, more motivated, and happier.

Lots of research backs up what Dr. Neff is saying, especially when it comes to teenagers. Studies show that teens who are kind to themselves - meaning they don't beat themselves up over every little mistake - tend to feel less stressed out and more satisfied with life. Plus, they're braver about trying new things, they don't get bogged down by mistakes, and they bounce back faster when things don't go their way.

Trying to be perfect is like being stuck on a hamster wheel - it's exhausting and gets us nowhere. This constant chase can lead to feeling really down and worried all the time, especially about what other people think of us. It can stop us from doing things we might enjoy or from learning new stuff because we're too scared of failing or looking silly.

But when we start being as nice to ourselves as we are to our friends, it changes the game. We start to see challenges as chances to grow instead of just potential embarrassments. Dr. Neff's idea is like having a superpower. It helps us deal with tough times without being so hard on ourselves, making life feel a lot smoother and more enjoyable.

Research shows that this kind of self-kindness doesn't just make us feel better; it actually makes us more open to trying new stuff. Teens who don't sweat their flaws as much are more likely to jump into new experiences, figure things out as they go, and not give up when things get tough. This means they learn more and get better at bouncing back from setbacks, which is a pretty big deal in handling life's ups and downs.

So, what all this science and research boils down to is pretty simple: chasing after being perfect is a waste of time. What really works for making us feel good and living a full life is embracing our mess-ups and quirks. It's about giving ourselves a break and recognizing that it's totally normal to not get everything right all the time. This way, we can actually enjoy life more, take on new adventures, and not get knocked down by the tough stuff for too long.

Practical Steps Towards Self-Acceptance

Starting to really like who you are, even the parts of you that aren't "perfect," can feel like a big journey. But it's totally doable. Here's how you can start walking down that path.

Talk to Yourself Like a Friend

First things first: think about how you talk to yourself when you mess up or don't do something perfectly. If you're being super hard on yourself, it's time for a change. Imagine if your best friend came to you feeling down about the same thing. You wouldn't be harsh with them, right? You'd be kind and supportive. So, why not treat yourself the same way? Next time you're being your own worst critic, take a pause. Ask yourself if you'd say those things to a friend. If the answer's no, then it's time to switch up how you're talking to yourself. Try to be more like a cheerleader for yourself, focusing on the good stuff and being understanding when things don't go as planned.

Writing It Down Helps

Journaling is like a secret weapon for getting to know and like yourself better. Spend some time each day, or even just a few times a week, writing down what's on your mind. Make sure to write about what you appreciate about yourself, too—not just the things you're good at but also the parts of you that you might not be so sure about. Writing this stuff down can help you see that what you think of as your flaws are actually what make you interesting and different. Plus, looking back on how these traits have shaped your experiences or helped you grow can show you why they're worth celebrating.

Find Your People

Feeling like you're the only one struggling with self-doubt can be lonely. But when you open up and share your feelings with others, you'll quickly realize you're not alone. Whether it's online, in a club at school, or just hanging out with friends, talking about your challenges (and hearing about theirs) can make a huge difference. It's comforting to know that everyone has insecurities and that we're all trying to figure out how to deal with them. Sharing stories and advice can help everyone feel more understood and less isolated.

By trying out these steps—being nicer to yourself, writing down your thoughts and feelings, and connecting with others who get what you're going through—you can start to feel more comfortable in your own skin. It's not about being perfect; it's about being cool with who you are, quirks and all. And that's a pretty great feeling.

Remember, the journey to self-acceptance is just that—a journey. It doesn't happen overnight, but with each step, each act of kindness towards ourselves, we light up the dark, turning our flaws into our most brilliant badges of honor.

Real Life vs Social Media

Social media is like a huge, buzzing digital world where we can keep up with friends, share what we're up to, and find cool stuff that interests us. It's pretty awesome to have so much information and so many connections right at our fingertips. But, there's a flip side to all this easy access and constant sharing that we don't always think about.

Researchers and psychologists have found out that spending a lot of time scrolling through social media apps can actually make us feel not so great about ourselves. Dr. Lisa Damour, who knows a ton about teenagers and how they think, talks about something called the "comparison trap." This happens when we start measuring our everyday life against the best bits that other people choose to share online. It's like we're looking at their greatest hits album while we're just living our regular life, and it can make us feel like we're not doing as well or looking as good as everyone else.

Take Mia's story, for example. She's 15, really smart, and super creative. But when she scrolls through her feed every night, seeing photos and stories of people looking perfect and having the time of their lives, she starts to feel down. She thinks she's not as interesting or good-looking as they are. And Mia's not alone. A bunch of teens feel like they have to post stuff that makes their life look amazing, even if it's not really how things are going. They feel like they need to hide the real parts of their lives that make them who they are.

This pressure to only show the cool, perfect side of life is a big deal. It can make us anxious about how we look and what we're doing compared to everyone else. But remember, those pictures and stories are just the highlights. Everyone has regular, not-so-perfect moments, but those usually don't make it onto social media.

Understanding that social media shows a filtered version of life is important. It helps us remember that it's okay to be ourselves, with all the unique, quirky, and sometimes messy parts of our lives. Those are what make us real, and honestly, that's way more interesting than any perfect post.

Understanding Filters and The Real You

So, you know how everyone seems to look perfect on social media? Well, there's a lot going on behind those flawless pictures. Filters and photo editing apps can turn a regular photo into something that looks straight out of a magazine. It's pretty cool, but it's also got a downside. When everything looks perfect online, it's easy to forget what real beauty looks like.

Think about it: when was the last time you laughed so hard your stomach hurt? That kind of happiness doesn't need a filter to be beautiful. But, here's the thing – a lot of us, especially teens, feel this pressure to only show the "best" version of ourselves online. The Pew Research Center did this study and found out that a ton of teens feel like they need to post pictures that make them look good all the time. It's like we're stuck in this loop where we're always comparing ourselves to others and trying to make sure our next post is even better.

This cycle of comparing and editing doesn't just stop with photos. It starts to mess with how we see ourselves and the world around us. When likes and comments start feeling like they're the only things that matter, it's easy to forget that there's so much more to us than what we post online.

Breaking out of this comparison trap isn't easy, but it's important. We've got to remember that real life isn't always picture-perfect – and that's totally okay. Real beauty comes from being ourselves, whether that's being goofy, making mistakes, or just hanging out in our sweatpants. It's about realizing that behind every polished photo on social media, there's a real person with their own stories and struggles.

Your flaws are not the enemy. They are not obstacles to be overcome but facets of your unique story. Like the *kintsugi* pottery, we are all more beautiful for having been broken, for having lived, and for having learned. As we embrace our imperfections, we step into a world where we're not defined by our flaws but enriched by them, where we recognize the beauty in the imperfect and celebrate the diversity of the human experience.

Drawing the Digital Line - Healthy Boundaries in the Social Media Age

In this world where our phones beep at us non-stop, making some rules for ourselves about social media isn't just a nice idea—it's super important for keeping us feeling good. Especially for teenage girls, who are right in the middle of figuring out who they are, setting these rules is about way more than just cutting down screen time. It's about making sure there's room in your life for growing, finding out more about yourself, and making real, meaningful friendships.

When your phone is always lighting up with notifications, it's super easy to get caught up in what's happening on your screen and miss out on what's happening right in front of you. By setting some boundaries, like maybe deciding not to check Instagram first thing in the morning or right before bed, you're giving yourself a chance to focus on other stuff that makes you happy and helps you grow. It's about choosing to spend your time on things that really matter and make you feel good about yourself.

For all the girls out there trying to navigate through high school and all the ups and downs that come with being a teenager, remember that managing how and when you use social media can really help you feel more in control. It's like creating a little bubble for yourself where you can breathe, think, and just be without worrying about what everyone else is doing online.

And here's the thing: when you start setting these boundaries, you're taking a big step towards valuing real-life connections over online ones. It's about learning that hanging out with your friends in person, getting lost in a good book, or spending time on hobbies you love can be way more fulfilling than any amount of likes or comments.

The Balancing Act

Think about trying to walk a tightrope. On one side, you've got all the cool stuff you can do and see online, and on the other, there's everything happening in the real world, like hanging out with friends or just enjoying a sunny day. Staying on that rope without tipping too far one way or the other? That's the big challenge.

Dr. Sherry Turkle, who's been studying how we interact online for years at MIT, tells us something pretty important: using technology changes not just what we do but who we are. It's a big deal because it shows how being online a lot can really mix up our sense of who we are and how we connect with people face-to-face.

So, how do we keep our balance? It's about making sure we're not getting so caught up in the online world that we forget to live in the real one. It means setting up some rules for ourselves about when and how we use our phones, computers, or gaming systems.

For example, maybe you choose to put the phone down during meals so you can actually talk to your family. It's all about finding ways to make sure you're spending enough time in the real world, too.

Creating these boundaries helps us take control of our tech use. It's like drawing a line that keeps our online activities from taking over our lives. By doing this, we make sure we're using technology as a tool to help us, not something that controls us or makes us feel worse about ourselves.

Remember, it's totally okay to enjoy being online and to use social media to stay connected. The key is to make sure you're also living your life offline, spending time with friends in person, exploring new hobbies, or just taking a moment to chill. Balancing our online and offline lives lets us enjoy the best of both worlds without feeling overwhelmed or lost.

The Power of Unplugging

Erica, who's in 11th grade, found herself stuck in a loop of scrolling through her phone and laptop every night, way past her bedtime. This habit was messing with her sleep big time. She'd stay up super late, only to wake up feeling like a zombie the next morning. Realizing this wasn't working for her, Sarah decided to try something new: she set a rule for herself to turn off all her gadgets an hour before she planned to hit the hay.

This small change made a huge difference pretty quickly. Tabitha started waking up feeling more refreshed and ready to take on the day. But the cool part? The benefits didn't stop at just getting better sleep. With her evenings free from the grip of her phone and laptop, Tabitha rediscovered old hobbies and interests she'd let slide. She spent more time hanging out and actually talking with her family, dove deeper into her schoolwork without the constant distractions, and picked up her paintbrushes again, reconnecting with her passion for art.

What Tabitha found out is actually backed by science. Research, like the study done by the National Sleep Foundation, shows that teens who stare at screens right before bed tend to have a tougher time falling asleep and don't sleep as well. It turns out, the blue light from screens messes with our brains, tricking them into thinking it's still daytime, which makes shutting down for a good night's sleep pretty hard.

But here's the deal: setting a "digital curfew" does more than just help us catch some quality Zs. It gives us a break from the non-stop buzz of the online world, letting our brains chill out and get ready for sleep. This kind of rest is super important because it helps us feel sharper, happier, and healthier during the day. Plus, it opens up space for us to get back into hobbies, spend real quality time with people we care about, and just enjoy life away from a screen.

Tabitha's story is a big reminder that sometimes, to really plug into what matters, we need to unplug from our devices. Making a rule to step away from screens before bed isn't just about getting better sleep—it's about making our lives more awesome, both online and off. It's about making sure we're living our best life, with plenty of time for friends, family, hobbies, and just being us.

Quality Over Quantity

Let's talk about how we use social media. It's not just about cutting down the hours we're online; it's also about what we're actually doing while scrolling. Dr. Jean Twenge, who wrote the book "iGen," shares some pretty cool advice. She says we should really think about how we're spending our time on our phones or computers. Instead of just mindlessly scrolling through posts, why not spend that time talking to our close friends or checking out stuff that really interests us?

Choosing to focus on meaningful stuff when we're online can totally change how we feel about social media. It can switch from making us feel bad about ourselves to helping us feel connected and inspired. Imagine using Instagram, Snapchat, or whatever platform you're into, in a way that adds something positive to your day instead of taking away from it.

By being picky about what we do online, we can make our social media time a lot more valuable. It's like choosing to have deep conversations with a good friend instead of just small talk with a bunch of people you barely know. This way, every time you log off, you feel better, not worse.

So, it's all about making smart choices. Do you want to end your day feeling down because you were comparing your life to someone else's highlight reel, or do you want to feel good because you had a great chat with a friend or learned something new? By focusing on the stuff that really matters to us, we can make sure social media is a tool that brings us joy and inspiration. Remember, social media should add to your life, not make it more stressful.

So, think about what changes you might want to make to keep your online and offline lives in balance. It's all about making choices that help you feel good and stay true to yourself, both in the digital world and beyond.

Things to Keep in Mind

- It's okay to take a break. You don't have to be online all the time. It's totally fine to turn off notifications or set times when you just don't check your phone. This way, you can have some quiet time for yourself or focus more on hanging out with people face-to-face.

- Make your feed a happy place. Follow accounts that make you smile or teach you something cool, and don't be afraid to unfollow or mute the ones that make you feel bad about yourself. Your social media should be a place that lifts you up.

- Remember, real life doesn't have a filter. Everyone has ups and downs, but people usually only share the highlight reel online. Don't let those perfect posts make you forget that it's okay to be perfectly imperfect.

- Choose Who You Follow Wisely. Make your feed a place of positivity. Follow accounts that make you feel good and are about realness, not just perfection.

- Set Boundaries for Social Media. Try not to be on social media all the time. Make sure to take breaks, especially before bed, to help you unwind and sleep better.

- Do More Offline. Spend time doing things that make you feel good about yourself, like hobbies, sports, or hanging out in person with friends.

- Be Kind to Yourself. Remember to talk to yourself like you would to your best friend. You wouldn't be harsh or mean to them, so don't do it to yourself.

- Talk About It. Sharing how you feel about social media pressure with friends or family can help. You'll probably find out you're not the only one feeling this way.

Chapter 3: Navigating Relationships

Friendships are like being on a big adventure where every giggle, deep talk, and chill-out time together builds up some of the coolest moments in life. When you're a teenager, these moments feel even more special because everyone is trying to figure out who they are and where they fit in. This part of the book is going to take a closer look at what makes some friendships feel like you've struck gold and how to spot the ones that might actually be bringing you down.

Think of your friendships as the ultimate squad, where being real with each other is what it's all about. True friends are those who make you feel awesome for just being you. They're the ones who cheer you on, no matter what, and are ready to ride out the tough times right beside you. These kinds of friendships feel easy and give back just as much as you put in.

But, let's be honest, not all friendships feel this way. As we all try to figure out who we want to be, sometimes we run into friendships that feel more like a chore than a cheer. Maybe you're always the one making plans, or you feel worse about yourself after hanging out. These are the warning signs that a friendship might not be the best fit. It's important to notice these signs early so you can decide what kind of friendships you really want to invest your heart in.

And it's not just about avoiding the not-so-great friendships; it's also about celebrating and holding on to the good ones. The friends who make you laugh until your stomach hurts, who love hearing about what makes you excited, and who are there to remind you of your worth when you forget—those are the keepers.

This chapter is all about figuring out the friendship map, learning how to navigate through the rough patches, and how to keep the good vibes going with your true friends. It's about making the most out of this wild ride called friendship, choosing the right companions for your journey, and making memories that last a lifetime.

What Makes Friendship Awesome

Finding a true friend feels like hitting the jackpot. It's all about having someone who really gets you, stands by you, and cares about what's happening in your life. It's like being on a team where everyone's rooting for each other, wanting everyone to win and be happy.

Let's talk about Maya and Zoe. Maya's all about art and standing up for what she believes in, while Zoe loves tackling tough math problems and diving into mystery novels. They're into totally different things, but that's what makes their friendship super special. They show us that friends don't have to like all the same stuff to be close. Actually, having different interests can make your friendship even stronger because you get to cheer each other on and learn cool stuff from each other.

In the best kind of friendships, you don't need to keep track of who's done more favors or who's been there for you more times. Everything just feels balanced and right. When there's a problem, you talk it out honestly, trying to understand each other's point of view and finding a way through that feels fair to both of you. It's about solving issues together and knowing that it's okay to agree to disagree sometimes.

These kinds of friendships are super important. They give you a sense of belonging and make you feel understood and valued just as you are. Having a friend who cheers for you when things go great and supports you when they don't is one of the best feelings in the world.

So, when you're building friendships, look for those connections where you can be yourself, share your dreams, and know you're supported. These are the friendships that last and make every day brighter. It's not about having a friend who's just like you but finding someone who respects you, shares your values, and is there for you, no matter what.

When Friendships Go South

Ever had a friend who started off as the coolest person you knew, but then things got weird and you ended up feeling pretty lousy about yourself? That's what happened to Samantha with her friend, Emma. At first, hanging out with Emma was all about fun and adventures, which sounded awesome. But as time went on, Samantha started to notice that every time she shared something good about herself, Emma didn't really seem happy for her. Instead, Emma would change the subject or, worse, make Samantha feel silly for even bringing it up.

Dr. Lisa Firestone talks about friendships like this, calling them toxic because they can make you doubt yourself and bring a whole lot of negativity into your life. It's like, instead of feeling pumped after hanging out with your friend, you feel drained and kind of down.

Samantha started to feel this way a lot. Whenever she did something cool or had some good news, Emma's reaction was pretty much a downer. And it wasn't just about not cheering for Samantha's wins. Emma didn't really listen to what Samantha needed or wanted. It was all about Emma, all the time.

This made Samantha feel stressed and low. She realized that spending time with Emma wasn't fun anymore; it was starting to make her feel bad about herself. That's a huge sign that a friendship isn't working out. Good friends are supposed to make you feel great, support you, and be happy for you when things go well. They should be people who listen and care about what's going on with you, not just themselves.

So, if you ever find yourself feeling down after hanging out with someone or noticing that they're not really there for you, it might be a sign to take a step back and think about whether this friendship is good for you. True friends should lift you up and make your life better, not harder. Remember, it's okay to move on from friendships that aren't making you happy. You deserve friends who cheer for you, listen to you, and make you feel good about yourself.

Handling Friendships: The Good, The Bad, and The In-Between

So, you've figured out which friends are keepers and which ones might not be so great for you. That's a huge step! But what comes next? How do you deal with these friendships moving forward?

With the good friendships, it's all about giving as much as you're getting. Celebrate the awesome stuff together, whether it's big wins like making the team or small victories like acing a test. And when things get rough, be there to help each other through. Sometimes, you'll need to have tough conversations. Maybe someone got their feelings hurt or there was a big misunderstanding. Talking these things out honestly can actually make your friendship stronger. It shows you both care enough to fix what's wrong and move forward.

Now, if you're dealing with a friendship that's more draining than uplifting, setting boundaries is key. Saying no is totally okay. If hanging out with someone starts making you feel bad more often than not, it's okay to take a step back and spend less time with them. You've got to look out for yourself, and sometimes that means walking away from people who bring you down. It's not easy, but letting go of negative friendships makes room for better ones to come into your life.

Letting go of a friendship doesn't mean you failed or that you're a bad friend. It means you're brave enough to choose happiness and peace over stress and drama. It opens up space for new friends who get you, support you, and make you feel good about yourself.

In all of this, remember: friendships are supposed to make your life better, not harder. The friends you choose to stick with should make you feel valued, respected, and happy. Whether you're cheering each other on, working through disagreements, or just hanging out and having fun, your friendships should feel like a two-way street.

So, take charge of your friendships. Keep the good ones close, work on fixing what can be fixed, and don't be afraid to walk away from the ones that hurt. Each friendship, no matter how it turns out, teaches you something important. Carry those lessons with you as you build the kind of friendships that light up your life.

Friendships: The Ultimate Adventure

Figuring out friendships is one of the best parts of growing up. It's like being on a journey where you learn a ton about being there for each other, understanding different points of view, and standing strong together. Getting the hang of spotting the good friendships from the not-so-good ones sets you up for some awesome times ahead. The key? Surround yourself with friends who lift you up and make sure you're doing the same for them.

Having true friends is all about that amazing feeling when someone totally gets you, shares your happiest moments, and helps you through the tough ones. It's finding those people who cheer you on, push you to be your best, and laugh with you till your sides hurt. Learning to tell which friends are keepers and which ones might be bringing you down is super important. It means you get to fill your life with more of the good stuff and less of the drama.

Being a great friend is a two-way street. It's showing up when your friends need you, really listening when they talk, and being their biggest fan, no matter what. It's about dealing with disagreements by talking things out respectfully and trying to see things from their perspective.

As you go through this friendship journey, aim to build connections that are all about mutual respect, support, and having a blast together. Go for friendships that make your life brighter, that challenge you, and accept you just as you are. These are the friendships that will stick around, through the good times and the bad, turning even the simplest moments into memories you'll always cherish.

So, as you keep meeting new people and making friends, remember to pick those who make your world a better place and be that kind of friend in return. This is how you create a friendship story that's not just worth telling but totally epic to live out. Aim for those amazing friendships that make every day an adventure and help you grow into the best version of yourself.

Why Speaking Up Rocks

Imagine yelling into a massive canyon and hearing your voice bounce back, loud and awesome. That's a bit like realizing how cool it is to speak up for yourself. Dr. Karyn Hall, a psychologist who knows tons about this, tells us that telling people what you need is really brave. It shows you believe you're worth listening to, you're clear about what you want, and you're not afraid to say it out loud.

Let's talk about Lily. She's a sophomore who's super into helping the planet. She had this idea to start a recycling program at her school but was kinda worried at first. What if everyone thought her idea was silly? But then, she got to thinking: her ideas are important, and so is her voice. Once she started believing in herself, she was all set to share her plan. And guess what? It was a hit. Lily's story teaches us that believing in ourselves is the first step to getting others to listen.

Lily put together her plan, making sure to explain all the good stuff that could come from recycling at school—like helping the environment and getting students to think more about being green. When she shared her idea with teachers and classmates, they were all for it. They even helped her get the program started. It was a big win for Lily and showed that one person speaking up can really make a difference.

Lily's journey shows us something important: When you trust that your ideas and feelings matter, you can stand up and make cool things happen, not just for you but for everyone around you. Learning to speak up for yourself is about knowing your value and being brave enough to share your thoughts. It's a skill that can change your life, helping you to chase your dreams and stand up for what you believe in.

The Tough Parts of Speaking Up

Talking about what you really think and need can be super tricky, especially for teen girls. It feels like society is always giving mixed signals. On one hand, you're told to be strong and speak your mind, but on the other hand, if you're too upfront, you might get labeled as "bossy" or too much. This can make it really confusing to know how to share your thoughts without worrying about what people will think.

Then there's the worry about stirring up trouble. No one wants to be the person who causes drama or disappoints others, right?

But here's the deal: saying what you need and standing up for yourself is really important, even though it might feel kind of scary at times. It's a bit like walking on a tightrope. Sure, you might sway a bit and feel like you're about to fall, but keeping your focus on what you need and how you feel is what helps you keep going.

Imagine you're actually on that tightrope. The idea isn't to cross it without ever wobbling; it's to learn that wobbling is part of the process. Each time you speak up for yourself, it's like taking another step on that rope. You might not get it perfect every time, but that's okay. It's all about trying, learning, and getting better at balancing your own needs with the courage to express them.

Overcoming these challenges isn't about never facing them; it's about learning to deal with them in a way that works for you. Each time you manage to say what's on your mind or stand up for what you need, you're getting stronger and more confident.

So, while it might seem daunting to speak up, especially when you're worried about being judged or causing a stir, remember that your voice matters. Learning to use it—not just loudly, but clearly and confidently—is part of growing up. It's about realizing that even though you can't control how others react, you have the power to express your needs and opinions. And that's a pretty big deal.

Mastering the Art of Self-Advocacy

Learning to effectively advocate for yourself is akin to mastering any new skill. It requires patience, dedication, and yes, you're likely to encounter a few bumps along the way. But the journey to self-advocacy is incredibly rewarding, offering a path to greater self-confidence and personal fulfillment. Below, you'll find detailed strategies to help sharpen your self-advocacy skills:

1. **Embrace Your Worth**: Central to the art of self-advocacy is the deep-seated belief in your own value. This is not about ego but about recognizing that your thoughts, opinions, and needs hold weight. Acknowledge that you deserve to be heard and respected. When you start from a place of self-respect, you naturally communicate more effectively because you understand that what you have to say matters. This conviction serves as the foundation upon which all other self-advocacy skills are built.

2. **Clarify Your Needs**: Before you can advocate for yourself, you need to know precisely what you're advocating for. Take the time to reflect on your own needs, desires,

and the outcomes you're seeking. Are you asking for more support in a project? Do you need clearer boundaries in a relationship? Identifying your needs with clarity allows you to articulate them more effectively to others, reducing misunderstandings and increasing the likelihood of achieving your desired outcome.

3. **Assertiveness vs. Aggression**: There's a fine line between being assertive and being aggressive. Assertiveness is about expressing your needs and feelings confidently and respectfully, without undermining the rights of others. It involves active listening, open communication, and the use of "I" statements to express how you feel without placing blame. On the other hand, aggression often involves bulldozing over others' needs, which can lead to conflict and resentment. Striking the right balance ensures that you stand up

for yourself while maintaining healthy, respectful relationships.

4. **Build Your Support System**: No one is an island, and having a robust support system can significantly enhance your self-advocacy efforts. Friends, family members, teachers, or mentors who understand and support your goals can offer advice, encouragement, and sometimes even direct assistance. Surround yourself with people who believe in you and are willing to stand by you as you navigate the challenges of advocating for yourself.

5. **Embrace Setbacks as Learning Opportunities**: Despite your best efforts, there will be times when things don't go as planned. You might face rejection or encounter resistance. It's crucial to view these moments not as failures but as valuable learning experiences. Each setback teaches you something about negotiation, resilience,

and the complex dynamics of human relationships. By reflecting on what didn't work, you can adjust your approach and strategies for the future, continually refining your self-advocacy skills.

Mastering self-advocacy is a journey that empowers you to take control of your life, ensuring that your needs and desires are not overlooked but are actively pursued. With practice, patience, and persistence, you'll find that your ability to advocate for yourself improves, opening doors to new opportunities and fostering a sense of autonomy and confidence that will serve you well throughout your life.

Making friends and building a group of people who've got your back is kind of like learning a dance where no one's quite sure of the steps. It's a bit tricky at times, but also one of the most exciting parts of being a teenager. This chapter is like your dance guide, helping you find your groove in making friends and creating a support system that cheers you on, helps you grow, and sticks by you through thick and thin.

The Basics of Friendship

Every awesome friendship has a few key ingredients: respect, trust, and real care for each other. Think of these like the essentials for a friendship to thrive, kind of like sunlight, water, and good soil for a plant. Dr. Miriam Kirmayer, who knows a ton about friendships, says being yourself is super important. It lets people know they can be themselves around you, too. This sets the stage for friendships that go deeper than just hanging out.

Planting the Seeds: How to Build Your Crew

To start growing your friendship garden, you need to know what you're looking for in a friend and understand your own interests. Here's how to get started:

1. **Jump Into Activities**: Dive into clubs or groups that match up with what you love doing. Whether it's sports, art, helping the environment, or coding, these are the places you'll meet people who get excited about the same stuff you do.

2. **Embrace Different Kinds of Friends**: A garden with all the same flowers isn't as cool as one with tons of variety. It's the same with friends. Getting to know people from different backgrounds or with different views can make your life way more interesting.

3. **Keep Those Friendships Growing**: Just like a garden needs water and care, friendships need time and effort. Be there for

your friends, check in on them, and show that you really care about what's happening in their lives.

4. **Talk It Out**: Good communication is key. Be honest about how you're feeling, listen to your friends, and work through any disagreements with kindness and understanding.

Weeding Out Problems

Sometimes, friendships hit rough patches, just like gardens can get weeds. Jealousy, misunderstandings, or just drifting apart can happen. The trick is to deal with these issues early. Talk about what's bothering you, try to see things from the other person's perspective, and remember, it's okay to take a step back from friendships that make you feel bad more often than they make you feel good.

Enjoying the Friendship Garden

The real win isn't about having tons of friends; it's about having meaningful relationships. These are the friends who make you laugh, who give you great advice, and who accept you just as you are. This kind of support system is priceless. It gives you strength, helps you keep going when things get tough, and celebrates with you when things are great.

Friendship is a journey with ups and downs, but it's one of the best parts of life. By putting yourself out there, being a good friend in return, and choosing to spend time with people who make you feel valued, you're on your way to building friendships that can last a lifetime. So, as you navigate the dance of making friends, remember to enjoy the music, learn from the missteps, and celebrate every moment of connection.

Chapter 4: Overcoming Loneliness

Feeling like you don't quite fit in can be like walking through a huge, unfamiliar forest where it seems like everyone else has a clear path except you. This chapter is all about exploring that feeling—like you're on the outside looking in, trying to find where you belong. We're going to dig into why feeling different isn't just tough but can also be the start of an amazing adventure to discovering who you really are.

Being a teen is tricky. You're figuring out who you are, what you like, and how you fit into this big, wide world. Sometimes, it can feel like everyone else has it all figured out, and you're the only one left behind. But here's a secret: a lot of people feel this way, even if it doesn't look like it from the outside.

Experts on growing up and making friends, like Dr. Brené Brown, tell us that feeling connected to others is super important. But they also say that being true to yourself is what really helps you find your tribe—people who get you and like you just as you are. This chapter will show you that being different isn't a bad thing; it's actually what makes you special and can lead you to some pretty cool places and friendships.

We'll share stories about kids who've felt just like you do now—left out or alone—but found their way by sticking to what they love and who they are. Like the kid who was obsessed with comic books and felt super alone until he found a group of friends online who loved comics as much as he did. Or the girl who felt weird because she liked coding more than makeup, but then she joined a coding club and met her best friends.

Here's the deal: Finding where you fit in might take some time and a bit of courage to try new things. It's okay to be scared of standing out or worried about what other people think. That's part of figuring it all out. But don't forget to be kind to yourself along the way. Remind yourself that what you think and feel is important, and there's a place for you in this world.

Sometimes, making friends and finding your crew means looking in places you haven't thought of yet. Joining clubs, teams, or online groups that share your interests can be a game-changer. It's not about how many friends you have but finding a few people who really understand you. And remember, it's totally okay if things don't work out the first time. Every experience teaches you something new and gets you one step closer to where you want to be.

So, as we dive into this chapter, think of it as your guide through the forest. It's here to show you that even if you feel like an outcast now, there's a path for you that leads to amazing friendships and a place where you belong. Your unique qualities aren't just quirks; they're your strengths, and they'll help you find your way to a crowd that cheers for you just as loudly as you'll cheer for them.

Feeling Like an Outcast: The Landscape of Belonging

Belonging is something we all crave, kind of like how we need air to breathe or water to drink. It's super important, especially when you're a teenager. For a lot of us, finding our spot, where we really fit in, feels like searching for a hidden treasure. Dr. Brené Brown, who's spent a lot of time studying how people connect, says that wanting to belong is natural. We all want to be part of something bigger than just ourselves. But sometimes, trying to find where we belong can make us do funny things, like hiding what we're really into or changing bits of ourselves to fit in better.

Imagine you love drawing comic books, but you're worried your friends will think it's nerdy, so you keep it a secret. Or maybe you have opinions that are different from most people you know, so you keep quiet to avoid standing out. Trying to blend in this way can end up feeling pretty lonely, almost like you're sidelining the real you to be part of the crowd. It's a weird kind of alone, feeling distant because you're not showing everyone who you truly are.

This whole belonging thing can be tricky. It's about finding a group where you don't just squeeze in but where you can be your full, true self. The challenge isn't just about getting others to accept you; it's also about accepting yourself. It means looking for places and people who get you, where you don't have to pretend to be someone else to be liked.

Finding where you belong isn't just about looking around you; it's also about looking inside you. It's figuring out who you are and what makes you, you. And then, it's about sticking to that, even when you're tempted to cover it up to fit in. True belonging is when you don't have to change who you are to be part of something. It's finding those friends or that club where your real self is the best version of you there is.

So, as you're trying to navigate through finding your place, remember it's a journey. It's about balancing being true to yourself and connecting with others. And when you find those people or places where you can be your whole self, it's like hitting the jackpot. It's about making real connections that feel good because you're being genuine, and that's what true belonging is all about.

The Story of Chloe

Let's talk about Chloe's adventure. Chloe's always been the kind of person who looks at a toaster and wonders, "How does this thing actually toast bread?" While everyone else in her grade was chatting about the latest fashion trends or which celebrity did what, Chloe was way more into gadgets and figuring out how they worked. She was the girl who'd rather take apart her remote control car to see what's inside than go shopping for clothes. Because of this, Chloe often felt like she was on her own little island at school, different from everyone else because her interests didn't match up with what was "cool" for girls her age.

But then, something awesome happened. Chloe found out about a robotics club at a school nearby. It was like discovering a secret door to a place where people got her. This club was all about building robots and making them do cool stuff, which was right up Chloe's alley. For the first time, Chloe was in a room full of people who didn't think her love for tech was weird. Instead, they thought it was cool.

Joining the robotics club was a game-changer for Chloe. She didn't have to pretend to be interested in stuff she didn't care about just to fit in. Here, she could talk all she wanted about circuits, programming, and all the techy stuff she loved, and people listened. They even asked her for advice. Chloe had found her crew, a group of friends who shared her passion for technology and innovation.

Chloe's story really shows us that sometimes the things we think make us odd are actually what can lead us to where we really belong. It's all about finding those people who appreciate you for you, not for who you think you're supposed to be. And Chloe's adventure teaches us that there's a place and a group for everyone, no matter what you're into. You just have to keep looking until you find your spot, just like Chloe did with her robotics club. It's a reminder that even if you feel like you're the only one in your school who's into what you're into, there's a community out there where you'll fit right in.

Embracing Solitude: Enjoying Your Own Company

Being a teenager is like being on a non-stop social rollercoaster. There's always something buzzing, someone texting, and it feels like you've got to stay plugged in 24/7. But what about just chilling with the one person who's going to be there through it all—yourself?

Think of solitude, or enjoying your own company, as hitting the pause button on life's crazy remote. It's a chance to step off the social treadmill and catch your breath. When you do, you start hearing your own thoughts a lot clearer. It's like when the music stops and you can finally hear someone at a party. That's when you really start to get what makes you tick, what fires you up, and maybe even what you dream about when you let your mind wander.

Spending time alone isn't about being lonely or bored. It's the total opposite. It's choosing to hang out with yourself because, let's face it, you're pretty awesome company. It's during these solo adventures that you might find out you're really into writing, painting, or maybe even coming up with the next big app. Solitude is like the secret ingredient that helps your creativity and ideas grow.

And here's the thing about getting to know yourself better—you start feeling more confident in your own skin. Making decisions gets easier because you know what you want. You start to trust your gut more. That's empowerment, and it's something that sticks with you, making all kinds of challenges a lot less intimidating.

Finding happiness in your own company is kind of revolutionary. It's learning that you don't always need likes, follows, or being at every hangout to feel good. Happiness comes from knowing yourself, enjoying your own thoughts, and creating your own peace and quiet. It's about being your own best friend and liking it that way.

The Treasure of Solitude

Dr. Sherrie Bourg Carter, who knows a lot about how our minds work, says that spending time alone is super important, especially for teens. She believes that when you're by yourself, you get this awesome opportunity to think deeply, grow, and figure out who you are. It's like giving your brain the space it needs to breathe and stretch.

When you're always around friends or caught up in the noise of social media, when do you get the chance to ask yourself the big questions? Like, "What makes me happy?" or

"What am I really passionate about?" Being alone lets you dive into these questions without any distractions or worries about what others might think.

Learning to enjoy your own company is also a big step towards becoming more independent and strong. It means that you can face tough times without feeling like you absolutely need someone else to cheer you up or solve your problems. You start to realize that you're pretty good company all on your own.

So, solitude isn't just sitting around feeling bored, lonely, or sad. It's a golden chance to do some serious thinking about yourself, to get creative, and to build up your inner strength. According to Dr. Carter, making time for solitude is one of the best things you can do for yourself during these crazy teenage years. It helps you figure out where you're headed and what you want out of life, setting you up for a future where you feel confident and true to who you are.

Cultivating a Relationship with Yourself

Developing a strong, healthy relationship with yourself is like nurturing a garden. It requires time, attention, and care. Here's how you can cultivate this relationship, making it flourish and thrive through the power of solitude.

Carving Out Time for Solitude

Begin by consciously choosing to spend time alone. This could mean setting aside a peaceful hour in the early morning before the world wakes up, taking a thoughtful walk alone after school as the sun sets, or dedicating a portion of your weekend to solitude with your devices switched off. These moments are precious; they're opportunities for you to reconnect with your inner self, to listen to your thoughts without the interruption of external noise. It's about creating a sacred space where you can be with yourself, undistracted and focused on your inner world.

Diving into Your Passions

Solitude is the perfect backdrop to explore what truly interests you. This alone time is your canvas; paint it with activities that light a spark in you. If you're drawn to writing, let your thoughts flow onto paper or a screen. If books are your escape, immerse yourself in stories that transport you to other worlds. Creative crafts, music, or even spending time in nature can be incredibly fulfilling. These activities aren't just hobbies; they're windows into your soul, offering insights into what makes you tick and bringing you joy.

The Power of Journaling

A journal can be a mirror reflecting your innermost thoughts and feelings. Make it a habit to jot down your experiences, no matter how mundane or monumental. Document your aspirations, the challenges you face, and the triumphs you achieve. This act of writing not only helps in organizing your thoughts but also tracks your journey of personal evolution. Over time, your journal becomes a cherished chronicle of your growth, a testament to your resilience and development.

Embracing Mindfulness

Incorporating mindfulness into your solitude can magnify its benefits. Practices such as meditation, yoga, or even mindful breathing exercises can anchor you in the present, helping to clear the clutter of your mind and bring about a sense of peace and focus. These practices teach you to observe your thoughts and emotions without judgment, offering clarity and a deeper understanding of your inner self.

Enjoying Your Own Company

Perhaps the most significant aspect of cultivating a relationship with yourself is learning to appreciate your own company, without the constant need for external entertainment or social interaction. Challenge yourself to be alone without defaulting to scrolling through your phone or binge-watching TV. In these quiet moments of simply being, you often uncover the most profound insights about yourself. You learn that solitude can be enjoyable and enriching, that your own company is comforting and enough.

Cultivating a relationship with yourself through solitude is a journey that unfolds over time. It's about discovering who you are beneath the roles you play in daily life, understanding your desires, and embracing your uniqueness. By following these steps, you create a foundation of self-love and self-acceptance that supports your well-being and guides you in forging meaningful connections with others. Embrace the journey of solitude, for it is in these moments alone that you find the keys to unlocking the full potential of your being.

The Joy of Solitude

Starting to enjoy your own company isn't just about keeping busy when you're alone. It's more like becoming your own best friend— someone who's always there for you, patient, and kind. This friendship with yourself is super important. It's like the base for all your other friendships and teaches you how much you're worth, what you like, and how strong you are when everything is quiet around you.

When you're a teenager, life is a roller coaster of good times, tough times, friends, and breakups. Learning to be okay with being alone is like finding a secret spot where you can take a break, recharge, and come back feeling stronger and more sure of yourself. This part of your life is all about figuring out how to enjoy being alone. It's about valuing those quiet moments when you can think and get to know the amazing person you are.

So, embracing being alone turns from something that might seem lonely or boring into something that helps you grow, understand yourself better, and become emotionally stronger. When you get to be friends with yourself, it's like opening up a whole new part of your life where you can be real, be happy, and express yourself truly. We all can learn to love those quiet times, seeing them as chances to celebrate ourselves and the unique journey we're on.

Feeling like you don't quite fit in can be tough, but it's not something that will stick with you forever. Think of it as a sign saying, "Hey, maybe it's time to check out some new paths and see what's out there." The things that make you feel like an outsider? They're actually what make you special and can lead you to some amazing friends and achievements down the line.

Let's talk about Chloe. Her story is like a lot of ours. She learned that being different is actually pretty cool and that there are places and people out there who will totally get and celebrate you for who you are. It's all about finding where you truly belong without having to change a single thing about yourself. Being real and authentic—that's where it's at.

As we wrap up this chapter, keep in mind that your way of finding where you belong might look different from everyone else's, and that's perfectly fine. It's not about how easy or hard the journey is, but about having the guts to go your own way. Your interests, the quirky things about you, your dreams—they're like your personal compass. They'll guide you to the communities where you'll do more than just fit in; you'll totally shine.

Chapter 5: Cultivating Self-Confidence

Stepping Out of Your Comfort Zone

Starting something new and a bit scary is a lot like being at the edge of a diving board for the very first time. You can feel the chill in the air, your heart might be racing, and looking down into the water can be pretty daunting. But this moment, right before you decide to jump, is super important. It's when you begin to find out how brave you can really be and start building real confidence.

Now, let's talk about a girl named Luna. In class, she was super quiet, hardly ever speaking up, and when she did, her voice was so soft you could barely hear her. But one day, Luna made a big decision: she joined the debate team. Yes, the girl who used to stay in the background chose to step right into the spotlight. This was a huge change for her. At the beginning, it was tough. She would get nervous, mix up her words, and her cheeks would turn bright red. But Luna didn't give up. Instead, she kept going, practice after practice.

This part of Luna's story shows us something really cool about trying new things, even if they make us feel a bit scared at first. Every time we push ourselves to do something we're not used to, we grow a bit more. We learn that we can handle more than we thought, and that builds our confidence.

Luna's move from being the quiet girl to speaking up in debates wasn't smooth sailing. She had to face some awkward moments when things didn't go as planned. But it's exactly these challenging times that helped her become stronger. Each time she stumbled, she learned something new, not just about debating, but also about being brave and sticking with something even when it gets hard.

This shows us that stepping out of what we're comfortable with is really key to becoming more confident. It's about doing things that might make us nervous because that's how we learn more about ourselves and what we're capable of. Luna's story is a great example of how taking on challenges, and not backing down, helps us grow into stronger, more confident people.

Have you ever heard that trying new things can actually make you happier? It's true! When we push ourselves to do something different, it's like our brain lights up. It loves the challenge and gets busy learning from the experience, which ends up making us feel pretty good about ourselves. There's this smart psychologist, Dr. Angela Duckworth, who's done a lot of research on why some people keep going even when things get tough. She found out that building confidence is all about stepping up to challenges. You might not get it right the first time, or even the second, but it's all about keeping at it and getting a little bit better each time you try.

But what happens if you take that leap and things don't work out? That's where we need to have a chat about failure. Instead of thinking of failure as a huge roadblock, it's better to see it as just a small bump in the road. It's not there to stop you; it's there to help you find a new way to keep moving forward. Take Mia, for example. She didn't win her first debate, or her second, but she didn't give up. With every try, she got a bit better, learned a bit more, and slowly but surely, her confidence started to grow.

And don't forget how important it is to have people around who support you—friends, family, or maybe a favorite teacher. They're like your personal cheerleading team, always there to encourage you, even when you're doubting yourself. This kind of support is priceless. It can give you the extra nudge you need to try something that feels a bit scary or out of reach.

The big lesson here? Getting out of your comfort zone is key to finding out what you're really capable of. It's about facing those moments that make you a little nervous, the kind that make your heart beat faster just thinking about them. That's where the real growth happens. Think about all the famous people you know, from sports stars to your favorite artists. They all had to start with that first scary step of trying something new, of not letting fear hold them back.

Eleanor Roosevelt once shared some pretty wise words: "You gain strength, courage, and confidence by every experience in which you really stop to look fear in the face... You must do the thing you think you cannot do." What she's saying is super important for us. Facing our fears doesn't just help us get over them; it makes us stronger, braver, and more confident in everything we do.

Stepping out and doing something that feels a bit risky might sound tough, but it's actually really exciting. Every challenge you decide to take on is like a step on the journey to becoming an even cooler version of yourself.

And remember, every big name out there had to deal with being scared and facing challenges head-on. They managed to push through, and look where they ended up!

So let's make a promise to ourselves to not let fear decide what we can and can't do. Let's be open to new experiences, ready to face challenges, and willing to push a little further each time. By doing this, we're not just getting over our fears; we're on our way to building a ton of confidence. Let's take this journey together, one brave step at a time, and see just how amazing we can become.

Trusting Yourself: Believing in Your Abilities

Let's keep it real. Feeling a bit shaky or unsure when you're stepping into new territory is totally okay. It doesn't mean you're not brave or that you can't handle it. Dr. Kyla Haimovitz, who's pretty smart about how we learn and grow, tells us that facing new challenges is actually the first step in believing in ourselves. She says it's perfectly fine to feel scared. The key thing is to remember that deep down, you've got everything you need to tackle those fears head-on.

Dr. Haimovitz wants us to understand that being nervous is part of the adventure. It shows that what you're about to do is important and a little bit challenging. That's how we grow. When we decide to face our fears and do the thing anyway, we're proving to ourselves that we're stronger and more capable than we thought. It's like each time you push past that fear, you're telling yourself, "Hey, I've got this."

So, feeling jittery about trying something new? That's just your body's way of getting ready for the big leap. It's not just about overcoming that fear; it's about embracing it and moving forward anyway. Dr. Haimovitz's advice is pretty clear: dive into those challenges. It's in doing the things that scare us a bit that we find out how truly amazing we are. Each challenge is a chance to learn more about what makes you, you — and how much you can really achieve.

There's this girl, Amara, who was super scared of public speaking. Amara's story is one that might feel pretty familiar to a lot of us. The thought of speaking in front of her class freaked her out big time. Just imagining all those eyes on her made her want to run and hide. But then, something cool happened. Amara got a chance to lead a project on something she was really into, something that mattered to her a lot. Even though she was super nervous, she didn't back down. Her first time up in front of everyone wasn't smooth sailing—she mixed up her words and felt super jittery. But here's the kicker: she didn't give up.

With every chance she got to speak, Amara felt a bit more sure of herself. That giant wave of nerves began to shrink, turning into just a ripple. This didn't happen all at once. It took time and a bunch of tries, but slowly, Amara started believing in herself a bit more with each speech she gave.

And guess what? This isn't just something that happened to Amara. There's a bunch of research out there that says when teens like us take on new stuff and push through tough challenges, we end up feeling stronger and more confident. It's like every time you try something that scares you, you're actually building up this inner voice that says, "Yeah, I've got this!"

This whole idea is backed up by science. When we step out of our comfort zones and tackle something new, it does something pretty awesome to our confidence levels. It's not about nailing it every single time; it's about the guts to go for it and the grit to keep going, even when things get tough.

So, Amara's story and all this research really boil down to one big idea: facing our fears and trying new things isn't just about getting over those fears. It's about proving to ourselves that we're capable of more than we ever thought possible. Every new challenge is a chance to see just how much you can do. And that's a pretty cool way to build confidence, one step at a time.

Gaining trust in yourself when you're staring down something totally new can seem pretty tough. But there's a secret to making it feel a lot less overwhelming: start with baby steps.

Think about it like this: if you're freaked out by the idea of giving a speech in front of the whole school, try speaking up in smaller groups first. Every time you manage to do it, even if it's just saying a couple of words, give yourself a little cheer. These small victories are super important because they slowly build up your confidence, showing you that, hey, maybe this isn't as scary as it seems.

Carol Dweck, a really smart psychologist, came up with this cool idea called a "growth mindset." It's all about looking at challenges not as these giant walls you can't get over but as chances to get better and learn something new. She tells us to see the tough stuff as opportunities to grow. So, when something feels hard, instead of thinking you can't do it, try thinking of it as a chance to improve.

Having folks around who've got your back is also a big deal. It's awesome to have friends, family, or maybe a favorite teacher who cheers you on and gives you pointers on how to do better. When you know there are people rooting for you, stepping out of your comfort zone doesn't feel quite so intimidating.

And here's something really important: always remember to be kind to yourself for every step you take forward, no matter how tiny it might seem. Each time you try something new, you're actually strengthening your "I can do this" muscle, proving to yourself bit by bit what you're capable of.

Wrapping things up, it's super important to remember that trusting yourself when you're about to try something new doesn't mean you expect to nail it every single time. It's really about having the guts to just go for it and do your best, knowing that you're going to end up more confident and learn a ton about yourself with each try. So, don't be scared to jump into new stuff. You totally got this!

When you're standing there, thinking about doing something you've never done before, remember it's not about being perfect. It's about trying, learning, and getting better. Every attempt, even if it doesn't work out the way you hoped, teaches you something valuable and gets you one step closer to being the awesome person you're becoming.

So, take a deep breath and dive into those new challenges head-on. Be curious, be open to making mistakes, and most importantly, be ready to learn from them. Every new experience is a part of your journey, adding up to make you stronger, smarter, and cooler than you were before.

You're ready for this. With a little bit of courage and a whole lot of heart, there's nothing you can't face. So go ahead, take the leap into all those exciting new experiences waiting for you. You've got this, and the adventure is just beginning.

Celebrating Achievements: Recognizing Your Strengths

The teenage years are a crazy mix of schoolwork, friendships, and big personal changes. With so much going on, it's easy to forget to stop and celebrate when we do something awesome. But here's why it's super important to make some noise about your wins: it does wonders for how you feel about yourself and helps you grow into who you're meant to be.

When you take a moment to celebrate what you've achieved, you're doing more than just having a good time. You're actually telling yourself, "Hey, I did something great, and I can do it again!" This builds up your confidence and helps you believe in yourself more. Each time you recognize your own success, you're teaching yourself that your hard work pays off, and that's a big deal—it keeps you motivated and pushing forward.

Celebrating helps you handle the tough stuff better. The happiness you get from celebrating makes the stressful times a little easier to manage. It's like filling up a tank of good vibes that you can tap into when things get rocky.

Plus, celebrating isn't just about feeling good in the moment. It's a key part of growing up and reaching your potential. When you acknowledge the good stuff you've done, you start to see more clearly what you're capable of, and you set yourself up for even bigger things in the future.

Carol Dweck, a famous psychologist who studies how our attitudes affect our success, tells us that when we take time to celebrate what we've accomplished, it helps us build a "growth mindset." This means we start to believe more in the power of our own efforts and see our hard work paying off, which encourages us to keep pushing and keep trying, no matter what.

Celebrating our successes does a lot for us. It makes the connection between hard work and great results super clear. When we see that our effort leads to success, it makes us want to keep going and tackle even bigger challenges. Think about it: when you've worked really hard on a project and it turns out well, taking a moment to celebrate makes you feel ready to jump into the next big thing, right?

Also, celebrating helps us stick with our goals, especially when things get tough. Every time we stop to recognize what we've achieved, we remind ourselves that we're making progress. This can be a huge motivator because it shows us that we're moving forward, even if it's just a little at a time.

Acknowledging our victories makes us feel good and satisfied with what we're doing, which is so important. It's like giving ourselves a pat on the back and saying, "Hey, I did that, and I did it well!" This not only keeps our spirits up but also fuels our drive to keep achieving.

Harper, a high school junior, always found math really tough. Every test felt like a huge challenge, filled with problems she thought she couldn't solve. Then, one day, she faced an especially difficult math test—something she was really worried about. Surprisingly, she ended up doing much better than she expected.

Instead of just moving on from her high score, Harper decided to really celebrate this win. She planned a fun night out with her friends, making a big deal out of her achievement. This wasn't just about having a good time; it was about marking her success and letting herself feel proud of all the hard work she had put into studying.

By celebrating her high score, Harper did something important for herself. She connected the dots between her effort and the good result, which helped boost her confidence. It showed her that she could do well in math and made her more confident to tackle future tests. Celebrating her success wasn't just enjoyable—it was a crucial step that helped her see her own progress and motivated her to keep pushing herself.

Harper's story teaches us a valuable lesson: small celebrations are not just fun; they're important. They help us recognize our achievements and encourage us to keep going. Celebrating helps turn a simple good grade into a milestone that can inspire us to keep working hard and facing challenges head-on.

Celebrating your wins does a lot more than just make you feel good; it actually brings people together and spreads happiness around. When you celebrate, you usually don't do it alone—you bring in friends, family, and maybe even teachers who have helped you along the way. This makes everyone feel more connected. These moments of celebration strengthen your relationships because you share the joy of what you've achieved. Plus, having everyone's support and positivity makes for a really great vibe, where everyone encourages each other to do well.

However, with all the rushing around trying to reach the next big thing, it's easy to think that stopping to celebrate might be a waste of time or a little self-indulgent. But it's important to shift how we think about this. Celebrating isn't about showing off—it's about recognizing the hard work you put in to reach your goals. It's a crucial part of achieving something. You set a goal, you work hard to meet it, and then you should take a moment to enjoy that success.

Experts like Dr. Angela Duckworth, who is a well-known psychologist and author, believe that celebrating our wins is super important, not just for the fun of it but for building what she calls an "emotional reserve." Dr. Duckworth explains that when we take time to celebrate, we're actually storing up positive feelings that can help us later on when we face tough times. This stash of good vibes keeps us motivated and pushing forward, even when things get tricky.

It's also really important to celebrate in a way that feels right for you. What makes one person happy might not work for another. For instance, if you love having quiet time, then chilling out with a good book might be your ideal way to celebrate a big win. But if you're someone who loves being around friends, throwing a small party or going out might be the perfect way to mark your success. The key here is to do what makes you feel truly happy and appreciated.

This personal touch makes the celebration more meaningful and enjoyable. By knowing what activities make you feel great, you can make sure your celebrations are genuinely rewarding. Not only does this make the good times more fun, but it also ensures that these moments leave a lasting positive impact, reinforcing the great feeling of achieving something and gearing you up for future challenges.

As we look at stories of teens like Harper who take the time to celebrate their achievements, we notice something really cool: they face new challenges with a lot more confidence. They believe in themselves and their abilities strongly. These stories tell us about more than just winning moments; they show how celebrating can set you up for even more success and good vibes in the future.

And as we wrap up this chapter, let's remember how every single success, no matter how tiny it seems, plays a big part in our life's journey. Celebrating these moments doesn't just make our own lives better—it also encourages our friends and family to celebrate their wins too. This can create a ripple effect, where everyone starts to feel more positive and supported.

So, let's make a promise to ourselves to take a moment to stop, reflect, and celebrate whenever we achieve something. It's a simple act, but it can have a huge impact on how we see ourselves and the world around us. By recognizing our achievements, we not only give ourselves a pat on the back but also show others that it's okay to take pride in their successes too. Let's keep this cycle of positivity going—it makes us all feel good and pushes us to aim even higher next time.

Chapter 6: Seeking Validation

The Art of Discernment: Navigating Opinions in Your Teen Years

Navigating your teen years is a lot like sailing through unknown waters where everyone seems eager to give you directions. Whether it's advice from friends, guidance from family, or tips from social media influencers, there's a constant stream of opinions on what you should do, how you should look, and who you should be. With so much advice coming your way, it can feel really overwhelming to figure out what actually works for you.

That's where learning to be discerning comes in—it's all about figuring out which pieces of advice truly line up with your own values and which ones don't. Being discerning means you don't just take every piece of advice at face value; instead, you think critically about whether it makes sense for you and your life. It's a crucial skill for any young woman who wants to confidently make her own way.

By developing the ability to discern, you empower yourself to sift through all the noise and make decisions that genuinely reflect who you are and what you believe in. This is especially important in a world filled with social media, where there's a lot of pressure to fit in or follow the crowd. Social media tends to amplify the most popular voices and trends, making it tough sometimes to stick to your own path without doubting yourself.

Ava, a 17-year-old high school senior, found herself in a tough spot when she got a college scholarship offer for athletics. It was a big opportunity, but it wasn't a simple decision. Her coach was all for it, telling her these chances don't come around often and pushing her to accept it because of the benefits it could bring to her sports career. On the other hand, her parents thought she should focus more on schools known for their strong academic programs, thinking about her long-term education and career.

Faced with these different opinions, Ava knew she had to figure this out for herself. She took some time to think deeply about what she really wanted for her future. She listed down her long-term goals and compared her passion for the sport with her interest in academic subjects. This wasn't just about choosing between two schools; it was about deciding what direction she wanted her life to go.

After a lot of thinking, Ava made a choice that felt right for her, not just something others wanted for her. She picked a path that allowed her to keep playing sports but also gave weight to her academic interests. This decision was hers alone, made after evaluating what was truly important to her. It showed she wasn't just following what someone else thought was best, but was making a thoughtful, balanced choice based on her own goals and values.

Developing the skill of discernment is super important for gaining independence, especially during your teen years when you're bombarded with all sorts of advice from different directions. Dr. Jane Brown, a psychologist who specializes in how teenagers behave, points out that being able to filter and analyze the advice you get isn't just about making choices—it's about building the skills you need to handle the complicated stuff life throws at you. Being good at discernment means you're not just choosing; you're choosing wisely based on a deep understanding of the situation.

Research shows that teens who get really good at this skill tend to feel better about themselves and are more confident when they need to make decisions. This boost comes from knowing how to pick paths that really fit who they are, which helps them feel more in control and sure of themselves.

So, how can you get better at discernment? Start by figuring out what really matters to you. Figuring out what matters to you, rather than focusing on what matters to everyone else, is a major part of developing self-love. What are the values you won't compromise on? Is it honesty? Loyalty? Creativity? These are like your life's guidelines. Once you know what's most important to you, you can use these values as a filter to sort through all the advice you get. This helps you keep what's helpful and ignore what's not.

Another great way to sharpen your discernment is to listen to lots of different opinions, even if they don't initially agree with yours. It's comfortable to stick with what's familiar, but hearing diverse viewpoints can really strengthen your ability to think critically. Try having discussions or even friendly debates with friends or mentors who see things differently. This not only broadens your perspective but also makes you think hard about why you believe what you do, which solidifies your own opinions and decisions.

Learning to trust your instincts is super important when it comes to making smart choices. Sometimes, the best advice doesn't come from others but from what you feel deep inside. Dr. Ella Sims, who knows a lot about how our intuition works, tells us that our gut feelings are really our brain's way of pointing us to what truly matters to us. Paying attention to these feelings is a big part of learning how to make the right decisions.

Discernment isn't about just blocking out what everyone else thinks; it's about knowing how to pick and choose which advice to listen to. For teenage girls, getting good at this isn't just about making smart choices right now—it's about setting yourself up for the future. As you grow and go through different experiences, each piece of advice you get and every decision you make helps you get better at figuring out what's best for you.

Remember, every time you face a decision, big or small, it's a chance to practice this skill. This isn't just about choosing what to do; it's about shaping who you are and who you want to become. By getting better at listening to your own instincts and carefully considering the advice you get, you'll find it easier to stick to your values and be confident in your choices, no matter what challenges come your way.

Learning how to choose the right advice helps you stay true to yourself during these formative years. It's about not just listening to what everyone else thinks is best, but also taking a step back, evaluating how this advice impacts your personal goals, and deciding if it's right for you. As you get better at this, you'll find it easier to navigate through life's challenges with confidence, knowing the decisions you make are truly your own.

The Illusion of Approval: Understanding the Pitfalls of Seeking Validation

Ever wondered why getting likes on your Instagram posts feels so important, or why a compliment from a friend can really make your day? You're not alone—this happens to a lot of people, especially teenagers. The reason we all crave approval from friends, family, and even strangers online is actually built into our brains.

During the teenage years, our brains pay a lot of attention to social interactions. Dr. David S. Yeager, who studies how teenagers think and feel, says that this isn't just about trying to fit in. It's about how our brains are wired to help us get along well with others. This focus on social relationships is something that has been part of human nature for a very long time.

Back when humans were living as hunter-gatherers, being part of a group was crucial for survival. Our ancestors needed their groups to find food and stay safe from predators, so naturally, our brains evolved to be really sensitive to what others think of us. This helped to keep everyone cooperating and sticking together. Today, even though we're not dependent on groups for survival in the same way, our brains still reward us for behaviors that make us feel connected to others. That's why getting a 'like' or a compliment can light up parts of our brain that make us feel good—it's a leftover from how our brains helped us to survive in the past.

Gabriella, who's 16, puts a lot of time into making her social media pages look perfect, always aiming to get more likes and comments. But even when her posts are successful, she often ends up feeling empty and stressed instead of happy. This is a common issue for many teenagers today. They think that to be liked and accepted by others, they need to only show the best parts of their lives online.

There's actually a scientific reason why social media is so appealing to teens like Gabriella. Studies show that when teenagers receive likes and positive comments, it activates parts of their brains that make them feel good—kind of like how it feels to win a prize or eat your favorite treat. This reaction in the brain is why getting likes can be so addictive and why so many teens keep posting to get more of that good feeling.

This cycle can be tough to break. The constant chase for more likes can make teens depend too much on what others think for their happiness, which can lead to feeling anxious or low when the expected reactions aren't met. Plus, this focus on getting approval online can lead teens to spend less time on real-world activities and face-to-face interactions, which are really important for their growth and happiness.

By understanding how social media works on our brains, teens can become more aware of its effects and start to manage their use better. This means finding a balance between their life online and offline, and making sure they're spending enough time on activities that make them feel good about themselves, not just what gets them more likes.

Depending too much on what others think can cause some problems, especially for teenagers figuring out who they are. Dr. Karyn Purvis, who studies how kids grow and develop, warns that relying too heavily on others for our happiness can make us uncertain about our true selves. If we're constantly trying to match what we think others will like, we might start to lose touch with what we really care about and what matters to us.

This is a tricky part of using social media for teens today. Sure, getting likes can feel awesome, but it's important not to let those external approvals shape how we feel about ourselves. The key is finding a good balance —having fun with social media while also staying true to what genuinely makes us happy, away from all the screens.

To keep a healthy view of social media, it's essential for teens to enjoy its perks but also make time for activities that they truly love, regardless of whether these activities are popular online. Diving into hobbies that really interest you can help strengthen your identity and make you feel more secure, no matter what people online are saying.

So, while it's nice to get positive reactions from friends online, it's crucial to also build up what makes you happy on your own terms. By focusing on what really brings you joy outside of social media, you can develop a stronger sense of self that isn't swayed by every like or comment. This helps maintain your well-being in a world that's always connected.

Why We Seek Validation Before Trying New Things - Releasing Fear of Failure or Embarrassment

The sensation of nervousness that creeps up when you're on the verge of stepping into something new is a familiar feeling for many. You might have found yourself hovering at the signup sheet for a new club, or hesitating at the door of a workshop where you could learn a cool new skill. That inner dialogue can be pretty loud, filling your head with doubts like,

153

"What if I mess up? What if everyone laughs at me?" This experience isn't unique to you; it's a common thread among many teens, particularly girls. It stems from a blend of self-awareness and the natural desire to fit in, which intensifies during the teenage years. As we unpack this, we'll explore the roots of why seeking approval and reassurance becomes such a critical part of navigating new experiences during adolescence.

"Studies have shown that girls, more than boys, worry about failing, especially in school and activities outside class. There seems to be a persistent notion floating around in our minds that we're somehow less capable than guys in areas traditionally dominated by them, such as math or sports. However, this is nothing more than a pervasive stereotype, and it's important to recognize that our abilities are not defined by such outdated ideas. We possess the potential to excel in any field or endeavor we choose to pursue, regardless of gender expectations.

Moreover, the apprehension about how others perceive us plays a significant role in our decision-making processes. The last thing anyone wants is to be tagged with unflattering labels like "dumb" or "weird" by peers. Dr. Rebecca Chen, a psychologist specializing in adolescent anxiety, points out that this dread of negative labeling can be paralyzing. It often prevents us from stepping out of our comfort zones because we fear the social repercussions of a possible failure. This cycle of wanting to engage in new activities but being held back by the worry of judgment creates a challenging barrier to overcome. It not only impacts our self-esteem but also limits our opportunities for personal growth and the satisfaction that comes with mastering new skills."

"So, what do we do? Often, the approach is to seek confirmation from those around us before diving into new endeavors. We might find ourselves questioning our friends to gauge their opinions on whether we should sign up for that new drama class or volunteer project. Or perhaps we seek the reassuring nod from our parents before we commit to learning a musical instrument or joining a sports team. This search for external validation acts as a sort of safety net, providing us with the comfort that should we stumble, someone will be there to catch us. And yet, the truly exhilarating part emerges when we finally make that jump—despite the fears and the doubts. That's when we often discover capacities within ourselves that were previously hidden. It's in these moments, after taking that risk, that we learn about our resilience and courage, surprising even ourselves with the strength we possess to overcome challenges and thrive in new environments."

So, how do we break free from fear? Setting out to conquer fear is like finding yourself on the brink of a massive, uncharted territory. It's especially daunting for teenage girls, where the dense fog of fear of failing or feeling embarrassed often clouds their vision, making it hard to see the road ahead to personal growth and self-realization. However, the means to dispel this haze are often already within their reach, hidden in their personal experiences, advice from seasoned experts, and the inspiring stories of those who have successfully traversed similar journeys.

Consider the example of Ella, a seventeen-year-old who was petrified by the mere thought of speaking in front of a crowd. Ella's adventure started in a very common place, one that many of us know well—the safe confines of her comfort zone, where the unfamiliar is kept at bay. Despite her initial fears, Ella took calculated steps toward her goal. She joined a debate club known for its nurturing environment, which proved crucial in her development. This club wasn't just about learning to argue points but about building a supportive community that values each member's growth. As Ella engaged more with the club, her self-confidence began to blossom. She found strength in her vulnerability, learning to channel her anxiety into a powerful motivator. Her journey through the realms of public speaking transformed her fear into a potent force that propelled her forward, ultimately helping her lead her team to victory at a national debate championship. Ella's transformation illustrates a critical point: overcoming fear isn't merely about getting rid of it but about reshaping it into something that pushes us towards greater heights of accomplishment."

Experts really believe in taking on challenges one step at a time. Dr. Karen Simons, a psychologist who knows a lot about teenagers, really supports something called "exposure therapy." She suggests starting with something small that still challenges you a bit. For example, you could throw out an idea during a class discussion. It's not too scary, but it gets you talking. Then, when you're ready, you could step it up and lead a group project. This isn't just about doing these things; it's about getting used to feeling a bit uncomfortable and learning it's okay. With each little step, you start to feel less scared and more confident because you see you can handle these challenges.

There's also some solid research that shows this approach works. A study in the *Journal of Youth Studies* found something pretty impressive: teens who slowly face their fears like this cut their anxiety in half after just six months. That's a big deal! It shows that when you take on little challenges and build up from there, you're not just getting over your fears—you're building up your ability to bounce back from tough situations in the future. This kind of step-by-step challenge is a powerful way to grow stronger and more sure of yourself.

"Peer support is essential in overcoming fears and trying new things. When friends are there to cheer you on, even the scariest tasks can feel a bit easier to tackle. Dr. Emily Rios, an expert in education, highlights the impact of positive peer influence. She points out that when one girl takes a brave step and succeeds, it not only boosts her confidence but also serves as an inspiring example to others around her. This can create a ripple effect, encouraging a whole group of girls to challenge their own fears and expand their horizons. The support of peers acts like a safety net, providing the emotional security needed to venture into new experiences. As friends root for each other's success, the collective strength of the group grows, making each member more likely to try new activities and take on challenges that they might have avoided otherwise. This supportive network is a powerful force, making it possible for girls to push through their initial doubts and discover their potential, fostering a community that thrives on mutual encouragement and shared successes."

Stepping Beyond Fear—A Guide for Teenage Girls

As each new day begins, so do the chances to tackle something new or challenging. For a lot of teenage girls, these opportunities can sometimes bring feelings of nervousness about possibly messing up or feeling embarrassed. But here's the good news:

these same moments are perfect for growing and finding out more about who you are. This section is like your personal guide to getting past those fears. It's packed with stories from girls just like you who have faced and conquered similar fears, advice from experts who understand exactly what you're going through, and the latest research to back it all up. We're going to walk through this together, step by step, so by the end, you'll feel ready to take on those challenges with confidence.

Step One: Acknowledge and Name the Fear

The first step on the path to overcoming fear is to acknowledge its presence. It's about confronting the fact that something makes you uncomfortable or scared. This act of acknowledgment is powerful because it shifts fear from being an undefined shadow lurking in the back of your mind to a clearly defined obstacle that you can address. Dr. Angela

Chen, who specializes in treating anxiety in teenagers, emphasizes the importance of this process. She points out, "When you identify what specifically scares you, you empower yourself to take control over it, turning it from a vague worry into a concrete issue that you can actively work on." This approach helps in demystifying the fear and lays a foundation for tackling it head-on. A practical example of this is seen in Leah, a high school sophomore. Leah always felt a wave of fear wash over her whenever she thought about speaking up in class. By acknowledging her fear of embarrassment and pinpointing speaking in class as the trigger, she was able to focus her efforts on this specific challenge. Naming her fear gave her a clearer understanding of what she needed to overcome and helped her devise strategies to confront and eventually manage her anxiety about classroom participation.

Step Two: Start Small

Taking the first steps toward overcoming your fears doesn't mean you have to dive headfirst into the deepest waters. It's all about beginning with manageable, bite-sized challenges that don't feel too overwhelming. Dr. Chen, a well-respected psychologist in adolescent anxiety, often recommends beginning with scenarios that pose minimal risk. This approach allows you to build your confidence slowly but surely. For instance, Layla, a student who previously struggled with speaking in class, chose to start by responding to questions she knew well. This boosted her confidence each time she spoke up without feeling threatened. Gradually, she began participating in more challenging discussions, venturing little by little beyond what felt comfortable. Each small success in these less daunting situations helped to diminish her overall sense of fear, paving the way for her to tackle more significant challenges. This progressive strategy proved effective in reducing her anxiety, making the idea of taking on larger tasks less intimidating and more within reach. By accumulating these small victories, Leah's journey illustrates how starting small can create a solid foundation of confidence, making it easier to face bigger and more complex challenges in the future.

Step Three: Develop a Support System

Building a support system is an integral part of overcoming any challenge, including the fear of failure and embarrassment. It's essential to surround yourself with people who not only understand your struggles but also offer encouragement and positive reinforcement. This network could include close friends, family members, teachers, or mentors—anyone who can provide a steady source of support and motivation. Having a robust support system in place makes it easier to face daunting tasks, as you know there are people who believe in your ability to succeed and who will stand by you regardless of the outcome. Layla, for example, found tremendous help from a teacher who recognized her potential and encouraged her at every step. This teacher provided her with practical advice and emotional support, which was crucial during moments of doubt. Additionally, Layla's friends were a constant source of encouragement, cheering her on and celebrating her small victories, which boosted her morale and fortified her resolve. This kind of support acts as a safety net, giving you the confidence to stretch further and try things that might seem too risky otherwise. It's about knowing that even if you stumble, you have a group of supporters who will help you get back up and try again."

Step Four: Use Positive Reframing

Think about changing the way you see your mistakes and those moments when things don't go as planned. Dr. Maria Gonzalez, a specialist in how our thoughts affect our feelings and actions, gives some pretty cool advice. She says, "Look at tough times as chances to learn, not just as failures." Imagine turning every challenge into a lesson. That way, whenever you try something new, whether it works out or not, you still win something valuable from the experience. This mindset can really change the game for you, making it less scary to jump into new activities or opportunities because you know no matter what happens, you come out learning something new.

Step Five: Practice Mindfulness and Resilience

Mindfulness might sound fancy, but it's really about finding ways to calm your mind and body so you don't feel overwhelmed. Techniques like taking deep breaths, meditating, or just sitting quietly for a few minutes can make a big difference. They help you pause and get your thoughts clear, which can be super helpful when you're feeling anxious. And then there's building up your resilience—that's all about getting stronger from each experience, good or bad. It means looking back at times things didn't go your way and finding what was good about them, what you learned, or how you grew. This doesn't just help you handle the tough stuff better next time, but it also builds up your confidence because you know you've handled tricky situations before and can do it again.

Step Six: Celebrate Every Step

Acknowledging and celebrating every effort you make is crucial, regardless of how minor it might appear. Each time you recognize your own efforts, you reinforce the confidence and pride that naturally develop when you confront and overcome your fears. Layla's experience serves as a great example of this practice in action. She decided to reward herself every time she participated in class discussions. This simple act of self-recognition not only lifted her spirits but also gradually increased her willingness to contribute more frequently. She might treat herself to a small snack or spend some time doing something she loved after school on days she spoke up in class. This consistent self-reward system didn't just make her feel better in the moment; it also built a positive feedback loop that made her more enthusiastic about engaging in class. Over time, this practice helped transform what was once a daunting task into a more enjoyable and fulfilling part of her school day, proving that even small incentives can lead to significant changes in behavior and attitude.

The Impact of Persistence

Sticking with these steps over time can bring about incredible changes in your life. A study highlighted in the *Journal of Adolescent Health* reveals that teenagers who regularly face their fears of failure and embarrassment see a big drop in their overall anxiety levels. This isn't just about feeling a little less nervous; it's about genuinely improving your quality of life.

This section has shown that the journey to conquer fears of embarrassment and failure doesn't have to be overwhelming. It's filled with small, achievable steps, the support of friends and family, and new ways of looking at old problems. Stories like Layla's shine as examples for anyone dealing with similar issues, showing that these challenges are not only manageable but can lead to profound personal growth. By sticking to these principles and facing fears head-on, teenage girls can move forward with confidence and resilience, ready to open new doors and explore the opportunities that lie beyond their fears. This approach doesn't just equip them to handle current anxieties; it prepares them for future challenges, turning daunting obstacles into stepping stones towards a more fulfilled and fearless life."

Relying on Your Own Approval: Embracing Self-Validation

Self-validation is all about recognizing and accepting your own feelings, thoughts, and actions as important and valid, no matter what anyone else says. This skill is super important because it helps you take control back from the outside world and put it where it belongs—with you. It strengthens your inner sense of self, making you feel more secure and less swayed by every comment or like you receive.

Practicing self-validation means getting to know yourself better and trusting your own feelings and judgments. It's about being true to yourself and feeling good about the decisions you make, even if they're not popular or understood by everyone else. This can make you feel more confident and independent because you're not waiting for someone else's approval to validate your choices or feelings.

By learning to validate yourself, you can face the pressures of social media and not be overwhelmed by them. You'll find that your happiness and self-worth come from within, not from how many likes your latest post gets. This shift doesn't just help you feel better now

—it also sets you up for a future where you can navigate through life with confidence, knowing that the most important approval comes from yourself, not from the outside world.

The Science Behind Self-Validation

Let's dive into why self-validation is super important, especially for teenagers. Experts who study how teens grow and handle emotions really stress how crucial it is. Dr. Samantha Klein, who knows a lot about teenage mental health, points out something pretty cool about self-validation. She says that when you, as a teenager, start to really believe in your own feelings and thoughts, you build up a kind of inner strength. This isn't just any strength—it's a deep power that doesn't get knocked down by the random stuff life throws at you. It's super important because it helps you develop emotional stability and resilience that lasts.

Research backs this up, showing some awesome benefits. Teens who regularly practice self-validation—meaning they really accept and believe in their own feelings—tend to have way less anxiety and depression. These are big issues that many teens deal with, so knowing how to affirm your own feelings can really help shield you from these struggles. Plus, these teens also feel happier with their lives overall. This boost in happiness probably comes from feeling more in control and confident about handling whatever comes their way.

So, learning to validate yourself doesn't just help you feel better now—it sets you up for a future where you're equipped to handle challenges more effectively. You get to navigate through the tricky parts of being a teen and later life with a lot more confidence and a clearer sense of who you are.

Practical Steps Toward Self-Validation

Embarking on the journey of self-validation involves a series of actionable steps that can significantly foster personal growth and self-confidence. Here are some practical methods to cultivate this crucial skill:

1. **Recognizing Inner Strengths:** The foundation of self-validation lies in recognizing and valuing your own strengths and achievements. It's about seeing and appreciating what you do well. A practical way to foster this recognition is by maintaining a daily journal dedicated to successes, no matter their size. Whether it's acing a test, helping a friend, or simply managing time effectively, writing these instances down reinforces a positive self-view and cultivates a

habit of acknowledging personal victories. This constant practice helps shift focus from external approval to internal satisfaction, strengthening self-esteem over time.

2. **Cultivating Mindfulness:** Developing mindfulness is about enhancing your awareness of the present moment, including your feelings and thoughts. By engaging in mindfulness practices such as meditation, guided imagery, or simple breathing exercises, you can learn to experience and accept your emotions without immediate judgment. This ongoing practice is vital for self-validation because it allows you to connect deeply with your feelings and affirms that they are important and real. Over time, mindfulness helps build a stable platform of self-awareness that supports all other self-validation efforts.

3. **Setting Personal Goals:** Establishing personal goals based on intrinsic motivation—goals that originate from your personal desires and interests—strengthens the practice of self-validation. For example, when Emily chose to improve her painting skills for her own enjoyment rather than for social media accolades, she was practicing self-validation. This shift to pursue activities for personal satisfaction rather than external recognition helps reinforce the sense that her own standards and passions are worthwhile. Achieving these personal goals provides a genuine sense of fulfillment and reinforces the belief in one's own capabilities.

4. **Seeking Constructive Feedback:** While the focus of self-validation is on internal approval, constructive feedback from trusted sources such as mentors, teachers, or close friends can also be valuable. It's important to use this feedback not as a validation of self-

worth but as a tool for growth and improvement. Constructive criticism should be seen as an opportunity to refine skills and strategies, helping you to align more closely with your personal objectives and values. This type of feedback, when received in a supportive environment, can enhance self-reflection and aid in the continuous development of self-validation skills.

Each of these steps plays a significant role in building and strengthening a sense of self-validation. By integrating these practices into daily life, teenagers can cultivate a robust sense of self that is anchored not in the shifting sands of public opinion but in a solid foundation of personal authenticity and self-respect. This skill set not only enriches the teenage years but also equips individuals with the tools necessary for a resilient and fulfilling life.

Chapter 7: Self-Care Is Self-Love

In today's world, where everything seems to move incredibly fast, self-care is like a safe haven for teenage girls. It's all about taking care of both your body and your mind, and in the process, building a deep, lasting love for yourself. In this chapter, we'll dive into just how powerful self-care can be. Plus, I'll share some easy, doable tips that you can start using today to help you on your journey to more self-love. By blending inspiring stories, expert advice, and practical steps, this chapter is your guide to starting a self-care routine that helps you grow in love with who you are.

The Foundation of Self-Care

Think of self-care as more than just an occasional treat for yourself; it's a regular practice that involves making choices to refresh your body, recharge your brain, and get you ready to handle whatever comes your way. Dr. Carol Richards, a psychologist who works with teens, describes self-care as purposeful actions aimed at keeping up and improving our physical, mental, and emotional health. If you're a teenager starting on this path, you might begin with simple but essential steps: eating nutritious foods, ensuring you get enough sleep, and staying active. These basics help maintain your health and build up your energy, making it easier to deal with daily stresses and bigger life challenges. By sticking to these healthy habits consistently, you lay a strong foundation for more complex self-care routines that can further enhance your well-being.

Real-Life Impact

Let's talk about Emily, a high school junior. Emily faced a really tough academic year filled with intense classes and lots of extracurriculars. At first, she tried to ignore her health and just focus on her schoolwork, thinking this was the way to succeed. But all this did was make her tired and less effective. Realizing this approach wasn't working, Emily talked to her school counselor, who introduced her to some basic self-care practices. She started to take short walks every day, which wasn't just exercise but a way to clear her mind. She also began doing mindfulness exercises, which helped her become more aware of her thoughts and feelings and less stressed. These changes might seem small, but they made a huge difference. Not only did Emily's grades improve, but she also felt happier and more confident in herself. This shows how starting with a few simple self-care steps can really transform all areas of your life, proving that taking care of yourself is key to doing well and feeling great.

<u>Expert Advice</u>

Experts consistently emphasize the importance of self-care in fostering a strong and healthy self-image. Dr. Carol Richards, an expert in adolescent psychology, explains the significance of prioritizing personal well-being, especially during the teenage years. "When girls learn to put their well-being first, they equip themselves with the tools to manage stress more effectively and to cultivate a robust sense of self-worth," she notes. This empowerment is particularly crucial during adolescence—a time of intense physical, emotional, and psychological changes. Navigating these changes successfully requires a solid foundation of self-care, which supports emotional resilience and promotes a positive self-perception.

Supporting Data

The value of regular self-care routines is also supported by substantial research. For instance, a study from the National Institute of Mental Health reveals compelling connections between self-care activities, such as regular exercise, and mental health outcomes among teenagers. According to the findings, teens who consistently engage in physical activities experience notably higher levels of self-esteem and significantly lower levels of depression and anxiety compared to their less active peers. Furthermore, additional research highlights the benefits of mindfulness and meditation. These practices are shown to positively impact adolescent mental health, leading to reduced stress levels and a healthier, more balanced outlook on life. Such studies confirm that self-care practices play a critical role in enhancing mental well-being, underlining their importance as part of a daily routine for teenagers navigating the complexities of adolescence.

Building a Self-Care Routine

Establishing a self-care routine may initially appear overwhelming, yet it can be approached in simple, manageable steps. Begin with integrating small, positive changes into your daily life. For example, you might start your day with a short five-minute meditation session to center yourself before the rush begins. Consider keeping a gratitude journal where you jot down things you're thankful for each day, which can shift your focus to positive aspects of your life and away from persistent stressors. Alternatively, allocate a few evenings each week to relax with a good book, opting for this instead of endless scrolling on social media, which often adds to anxiety. These small but significant changes can greatly enhance your emotional well-being. Additionally, integrating physical activities like yoga into your routine can do wonders. Yoga not only improves flexibility and strength but also contributes to mental clarity and emotional stability, helping you maintain a calm and focused mind amidst the chaos of daily life.

Community and Connection

The role of social connections in self-care is crucial yet frequently underestimated. Interacting with friends and family provides more than just fun times; it offers profound therapeutic benefits. These interactions help elevate your mood, improve overall health, and strengthen your emotional resilience. During challenging periods, having a robust network of supportive relationships can be tremendously beneficial. Moreover, engaging in community-oriented activities such as team sports or volunteer work can enrich your sense of belonging and purpose. These activities not only connect you with others but also reinforce your feelings of self-worth and contribution to society. The sense of community and mutual support gained through these interactions is a vital element of self-care, promoting not just individual well-being but also fostering a shared sense of collective health and happiness.

The Path Forward

As we explore real-life stories and listen to advice from experts, one thing becomes very clear: self-care is essential—it's not just a treat. It's crucial for building self-love and a strong, positive identity, especially during your teen years. For teenage girls dealing with all the ups and downs of growing up, getting into the habit of self-care is key. It helps you become tougher, more self-reliant, and leads to a happier, more rewarding life. By sticking with a self-care routine, you start to see your own value and learn to love yourself completely and without conditions. It's about committing to look after yourself every day, realizing how important you are, and gradually seeing yourself in a better light. Keeping up with your self-care routine ensures that your journey to self-love is ongoing, filled with personal growth, new discoveries, and lots of joy."

Chapter 8: Activities to Cultivate Self-Love & Confidence in Teen Girls

Journaling

Journaling is a powerful tool in the journey toward self-discovery and self-love. Through the simple act of putting pen to paper, you can explore your deepest thoughts, celebrate your personal growth, and navigate the complexities of adolescence. This chapter delves into a variety of journaling prompts designed specifically for teenage girls to foster a sense of self-love and acceptance.

These prompts are designed not only to engage you in the practice of writing but also to encourage a deeper exploration of the emotions, experiences, and aspirations that shape who you are. They offer a structured way to reflect on personal growth and foster a nurturing relationship with yourself. Each prompt is a stepping stone towards building a stronger, more loving relationship with yourself. As you continue to journal, you'll discover that each page not only tells a story but also weaves the fabric of your character.

Before diving into the prompts, consider establishing a routine. Journaling isn't about perfection; it's about consistency. Aim to write a little each day, whether in the morning to set the tone for your day or at night as a reflective practice. The key is to make it a habit, a regular part of your day that you look forward to.

Journaling Prompts to Explore Self-Love

1. **What I Love About Me:** Start simple. List five qualities you love about yourself. These can be physical attributes, talents, or aspects of your personality. Reflecting on these can boost your mood and self-esteem.

2. **My Proudest Moments:** Think about the times you felt proud of something you did. Describe these moments in detail. What did you do? How did it make you feel? Revisiting these memories can reinforce your sense of accomplishment and self-worth.

3. **Overcoming Challenges:** Write about a challenge you faced and how you overcame it. This prompt helps you recognize your resilience and capability to handle life's hurdles.

4. **Gratitude List:** Keeping a gratitude journal can profoundly impact your perspective. Each day, write down three things you're grateful for. This practice helps shift focus from what's lacking to what's abundant in your life.

5. **Future Me:** Envision where you want to be in five years. What are you doing? How do you feel? This exercise not only sets goals but also helps you connect with your hopes and dreams.

6. **Letter to My Future Self:** Write a letter to yourself five or ten years from now. What do you want to tell your future self? What hopes do you have for her? What advice would you give based on what you are experiencing now? This can be a powerful way to connect with your long-term aspirations and encourage yourself to work toward them.

7. **My Favorite Activities:** Reflect on the activities that make you feel most alive and joyful. Why do you enjoy them? How do they reflect your personal strengths or values? Understanding what activities fuel your happiness and why can strengthen your appreciation for your unique interests and talents.

8. **Compliments I Struggle to Accept:** Consider the compliments you find hard to accept. Why do you think that is? Explore what each compliment touches on—perhaps a hidden insecurity or an unacknowledged strength. Writing about this can help you see yourself through a more loving and accepting lens.

9. **Moments of Joy Today:** At the end of each day, jot down specific moments that brought you joy. These don't have to be big events; even small pleasures count. This prompt

helps to cultivate a habit of noticing and savoring the positive aspects of everyday life, reinforcing a positive mindset.

10. **The People Who Inspire Me:** Make a list of people who inspire you and describe what exactly about them you find inspiring. Reflect on whether these qualities are aspirations for yourself, and think about how you might embody these characteristics more in your own life. This exercise can illuminate qualities you value and wish to develop in yourself, fostering a sense of purpose and direction.

Movement for the Soul - Physical Activities to Foster Self-Love

Engaging in regular physical activity is another essential tool for building self-confidence. Whether it's yoga, dance, or team sports, exercise releases endorphins, which have mood-lifting properties. Physical activity is often celebrated for its health benefits, but its power to boost mental well-being and self-love among teenage girls is equally profound. Here are 10 diverse physical activities that not only strengthen the body but also nurture self-esteem and personal growth.

1. Yoga: Harmony of Body and Mind

Yoga is more than just physical exercise; it's a practice that integrates mind, body, and spirit. Dr. Anita Desai, a yoga instructor and psychologist, explains, "Yoga teaches acceptance and mindfulness, which are key components of self-love." Through poses and breathing exercises, girls learn to connect with their bodies in a gentle, nurturing way, promoting both physical flexibility and mental resilience.

2. Dance: Express Yourself

Dance allows teenagers to express their emotions and experiences through movement. Whether it's ballet, hip-hop, or contemporary, dance fosters a sense of freedom and self-expression. Emily, a high school student who joined a dance club, shares, "Dance lets me throw all my feelings out there. It's like telling my story with my moves. It's liberating and empowering."

3. Hiking: Connect with Nature

Hiking in natural settings not only provides a good physical workout but also helps connect with the environment. The tranquility of nature combined with the physical effort of hiking can be incredibly calming and grounding. Sarah, who organizes teen hiking trips, notes, "The girls often start the hike with the weight of the world on their shoulders and end with a sense of accomplishment and renewal."

4. Team Sports: Build Bonds and Resilience

Participating in team sports such as soccer, basketball, or volleyball can significantly boost self-esteem. The camaraderie and shared goals inherent in team sports provide a sense of belonging and accomplishment. Dr. Lisa Chung, a sports psychologist, states, "Team sports equip young women with the skills to handle wins and losses, fostering a resilient self-image."

5. Swimming: Fluidity and Strength

Swimming is a powerful metaphor for moving through life's challenges with grace and strength. It combines the rigors of a full-body workout with the soothing qualities of water. Grace, a competitive swimmer, says, "In the water, I feel both strong and serene. It's a space where I truly feel at peace with myself."

6. Martial Arts: Discipline and Self-Respect

Martial arts such as karate, judo, or taekwondo emphasize self-discipline, respect, and confidence. These practices teach girls to set boundaries and respect their own strengths. Mia, who practices karate, remarks, "Martial arts have taught me to stand firm, respect myself, and never underestimate my power."

7. Cycling: Explore and Expand

Cycling offers a sense of freedom and adventure, allowing girls to explore new terrains at their own pace. It's also an excellent way to increase stamina and independence. Zoe, an avid cyclist, finds that "each ride is a new adventure where I learn more about myself and my capabilities."

8. Pilates: Core Strength and Control

Pilates focuses on core strength, posture, and flexibility. It teaches control and precision with every movement, which can translate into greater self-control and body awareness in everyday life. Natalie, a Pilates instructor for teens, observes, "Pilates helps girls appreciate their bodies for what they can do, not just how they appear."

9. Running: The Runner's High

Running is not just a way to stay fit; it's also a path to mental clarity. The endorphins released during running can lead to what is often called the 'runner's high,' a feeling of euphoria that can lift the spirits and instill a sense of well-being. Laura, who runs track, says, "Running clears my mind. It's just me, the track, and my thoughts."

10. Gardening: Nurturing Growth

While not as intense as other physical activities, gardening involves bending, lifting, and using strength to manage plants and tools, making it a gentle way to stay active. More importantly, it allows girls to nurture life, see the results of their care, and connect with the cycle of growth and renewal.

Each activity outlined offers unique benefits that go beyond physical health, touching on emotional and psychological well-being. By engaging in these activities, teenage girls can cultivate a stronger sense of self-love, resilience, and a positive self-image that will empower them for years to come.

Giving Back to Grow: Volunteer Activities

Volunteering isn't just about giving your time and energy to causes or communities; it's a pathway to personal growth, self-discovery, and ultimately, self-love. For teenage girls seeking to enrich their lives and expand their horizons, engaging in volunteer work can be particularly transformative. This section presents a curated list of ten volunteer activities designed to foster a sense of achievement, community connection, and personal empowerment.

1. Animal Shelter Helper

Working with animals can provide immediate emotional rewards. Feeding, grooming, and playing with shelter pets not only helps animals in need but also builds empathy and a nurturing spirit in volunteers. Jessica, a high school sophomore, shares, "Helping at the animal shelter taught me compassion and responsibility—it's where I feel I make a real difference."

2. Community Garden Volunteer

Participating in a community garden offers a chance to connect with nature and contribute to sustainable practices. It's a peaceful activity that can improve physical health and mental well-being. Volunteers like Emma find joy in tending plants and contributing to their community's green spaces, "Seeing something grow because of your care is incredibly fulfilling."

3. Senior Companion Program

Spending time with elderly people in your community can be a deeply rewarding experience. Whether it's playing games, reading, or simply chatting, this interaction brightens the day for both the senior and the volunteer. According to Dr. Karen Simmons, "The intergenerational exchange enriches both lives, fostering an appreciation for history, wisdom, and resilience."

4. Youth Mentor

Being a mentor to younger children can boost your confidence and leadership skills. This role allows teen girls to serve as role models, guiding younger kids through academic activities or personal challenges. Sophia, who volunteers as a tutor, says, "Seeing my mentees succeed and knowing I had a part in that is incredibly empowering."

5. Food Bank Assistant

Helping at a local food bank can provide perspective on societal issues like food insecurity while contributing to the solution. Sorting, packing, or distributing food not only helps those in need but also cultivates gratitude and a broader understanding of community needs.

6. Environmental Clean-Up Crew

Joining an environmental clean-up is a proactive way to take care of the planet. Whether it's cleaning up local beaches or parks, participants not only contribute to environmental health but also gain a sense of global stewardship. Lauren, who organizes monthly park clean-ups, notes, "It's about taking action and seeing the immediate impact of your efforts."

7. Library Aid

Assisting in a local library can be a quiet yet fulfilling way to give back, especially for those who love books and learning. Volunteers can help organize shelves, assist in hosting events, or run summer reading programs for children, enhancing their organizational skills and their appreciation for literature.

8. Art Programs for Underprivileged Children

Working with art programs that cater to underprivileged children can unlock creativity and inspire both the volunteer and the participants. Creating art together allows for emotional expression and connection. Mia, an art program volunteer, reflects, "Art has a way of breaking barriers and opening hearts."

9. Disaster Relief Volunteer

Participating in disaster relief efforts can be a profound way for teenagers to engage with their communities during times of need. Whether it's helping rebuild after a storm, organizing donation drives, or providing logistical support, the experience can be life-changing. It instills a deep sense of solidarity and resilience as volunteers work hand-in-hand with affected communities. Ava, who volunteered after a local flood, shares, "The experience was tough but transformative. It showed me the power of community and the impact we can have when we come together in tough times."

10. Hospital Volunteer

Hospital volunteers get the opportunity to interact with patients of all ages, offering comfort, delivering messages, or guiding visitors. The experience can be eye-opening and profoundly moving, fostering a deep sense of compassion and a desire to pursue a caring profession.

Creative Expressions: Artistic Activities to Cultivate Self-Love

Art and creativity are powerful avenues for self-expression and personal growth. Engaging in artistic activities can help teenage girls explore their identities, express their emotions, and build self-esteem.

1. Painting and Drawing

Grab some brushes, paints, or pencils, and let your imagination run free on the canvas or sketchpad. Painting and drawing are therapeutic arts that allow for personal expression and introspection. Hazel, a high school junior, shares, "When I paint, I feel like I'm in a world of my own, and all my worries fade away. It's a space where I can truly be myself."

2. Writing Poetry or Stories

Writing is a profound way to delve into your thoughts and feelings. Crafting poems or stories helps articulate inner dialogues and emotions that might be hard to express otherwise. As noted by Dr. Helen Liu, a therapist specializing in adolescent creativity, "Writing provides a safe escape for exploring personal challenges and triumphs."

3. Playing a Musical Instrument

Learning to play a musical instrument like the guitar, piano, or violin can be incredibly satisfying. Music not only soothes the mind but also builds discipline and confidence. Rachel, who started playing the violin at age 14, says, "Music challenges me but also gives me a great sense of accomplishment when I master a difficult piece."

4. Digital Photography

Photography is a powerful tool for capturing perspectives and telling stories through images. Exploring your surroundings through the lens can help you see the world in new ways, enhancing mindfulness and appreciation for the moment. "Photography helps me connect with the beauty in everyday life," explains Nora, an avid amateur photographer.

5. Pottery and Sculpture

Working with clay or other materials to create pottery and sculptures can be a tactile and satisfying experience. These activities not only develop artistic skills but also provide a physical outlet for expression. According to art teacher Mrs. Jacobs, "Sculpting can be a grounding experience that brings one's focus entirely to the present."

6. Dance

Whether it's ballet, hip-hop, or contemporary, dance is an exhilarating way to express emotions and stories through movement. Joining a dance class can also be a fun way to meet people and improve physical fitness. Ellie, who dances weekly, finds it liberating: "Dance allows me to express feelings I can't put into words."

7. Fashion Design

Designing clothes or accessories offers a creative outlet for expressing personal style and innovation. Sketching designs, choosing fabrics, and sewing can be deeply fulfilling activities. Madison, a young fashion enthusiast, notes, "Creating something that I can wear is incredibly empowering."

8. Jewelry Making

Crafting jewelry allows for detailed and delicate creative work, which can be both meditative and satisfying. This hobby offers the joy of creating something unique and personal. Willow, who makes and sells her own jewelry, says, "Each piece is a reflection of my mood and creativity."

9. Culinary Arts

Cooking or baking is not only a life skill but also an artistic expression that involves senses of taste, smell, and sight. Experimenting with new recipes or decorating cakes can bring joy and a sense of achievement. Riley, who loves to bake for her family, shares, "Baking is my way of spreading love and joy."

10. Theater Performance

Acting in plays or musicals can be a transformative experience that boosts confidence and empathy. Theater also provides a supportive community where creativity and collaboration are celebrated. According to Ivy, a theater group member, "Acting helps me understand different perspectives and build confidence in public speaking."

Each of these activities offers a unique path to exploring personal interests and developing a deep, abiding sense of self-love. By engaging in these creative endeavors, teenage girls not only enhance their artistic abilities but also learn to appreciate their own uniqueness and value, fostering a healthy relationship with themselves that will support their emotional and psychological growth.

Your Journey Begins Now

As we draw the curtains on our exploration of self-love, let's reflect on the path we've traveled together. This journey, filled with growth, challenges, and discovery, has equipped you, the reader, with tools to cultivate a loving and compassionate relationship with yourself.

Self-love is not a destination; it's a continuous journey that evolves with every experience and decision. It's about acknowledging your worth and embracing your uniqueness, imperfections included. Dr. Lila Moore, a renowned psychologist specializing in adolescent therapy, articulates this beautifully:

"Self-love is the quiet acceptance of who you are. It is a perpetual practice that encourages us to treat ourselves with kindness and respect."

Throughout this book, we've explored various facets of self-love—from understanding self-talk and letting go of external validation to engaging in creative pursuits and physical activities. Each chapter has not only provided insights but also practical actions to integrate these practices into your daily life.

It's important to recognize that the road to self-love might sometimes be bumpy. You will encounter obstacles and challenges that may test your resolve. Embrace these moments as opportunities for growth. As you face these hurdles, recall the words of Dr. Moore, "Each challenge is a stepping stone on the path of self-discovery. Facing them with courage and resilience can dramatically strengthen your self-love."

No one is an island, and on your journey to self-love, the support of friends, family, and mentors is invaluable. Building relationships with those who encourage and uplift you can provide a network of positivity and support.

As you continue to grow and evolve, let the principles of self-love guide your decisions and interactions. Set boundaries that protect your well-being, pursue passions that light a fire in your soul, and make choices that reflect your self-worth.

This book has been a roadmap, and you, the bold traveler, have navigated its routes with openness and enthusiasm. The practices and principles laid out here are not just theories but tools for life—equip yourself with them daily. Remember, self-love is not just about feeling good; it's about recognizing your intrinsic value and treating yourself with the same care and respect that you offer others.

As you move forward, take with you the words of poet Rupi Kaur, "How you love yourself is how you teach others to love you." Let your journey of self-love be a radiant example that illuminates not only your path but also the paths of those around you. Here's to your continued journey—a journey marked by love, respect, and boundless potential.

Made in United States
Orlando, FL
11 September 2024

51405598R00120